GYMNASTIC EXERCISES FOR HORSES
Volume II:

Wow! It worked
Help! It didn't happen

by Eleanor Russell

© E & E Russell 2002

Edited by Richard and Frances Williams

Reprinted by permission

© Xenophon Press 2013

Xenophon Press Library

30 Years with Master Nuno Oliveira, Michel Henriquet, 2011
A Rider's Survival From Tyranny, Charles de Kunffy, 2012
Another Horsemanship, Jean-Claude Racinet, 1994
Art of the Lusitano, Pedro Yglesias de Oliveira, 2012
Baucher and His School, General Decarpentry, 2011
Dressage in the French Tradition, Dom Diogo de Bragança, 2011
École de Cavalerie Part II (School of Horsemanship),
    François Robichon de la Guérinière, 1992
François Baucher, The Man and His Method, Hilda Nelson, 2013
*From the Real Picaria of the 18th Century to the Portuguese School of
    Equestrian Art,* Yglesias de Oliverira and da Costa, 2012
Gymnastic Exercises for Horses Volume II, Eleanor Russell, 2013
Healing Hands, Dominique Giniaux, DVM, 1998
*Methodical Dressage of the Riding Horse, and Dressage of the Outdoor
    Horse,* Faverot de Kerbrech, 2010
Racinet Explains Baucher, Jean-Claude Racinet, 1997
The Écuyère of the Nineteenth Century in the Circus, Hilda Nelson, 2001
The Ethics and Passions of Dressage, Expanded Edition,
    Charles de Kunffy, 2013
The Gymnasium of the Horse, Gustav Steinbrecht, 2011
The Handbook of Jumping Essentials,
    François Lemaire de Ruffieu, 1997
The Legacy of Master Nuno Oliveira, Stephanie Millham, 2013
The Maneige Royal, Antoine de Pluvinel, 2010
The Spanish Riding School in Vienna and Piaffe and Passage,
    General Decarpentry, 2013
The Wisdom of Master Nuno Oliveira, Antoine de Coux, 2012
Total Horsemanship, Jean-Claude Racinet, 1999
What the Horses Have Told Me, Dominique Giniaux, DVM, 1996

Available at **www.XenophonPress.com**

GYMNASTIC EXERCISES FOR HORSES
VOLUME II:

WOW! IT WORKED

HELP! IT DIDN'T HAPPEN

by ELEANOR RUSSELL

© E & E Russell 2002

© Xenophon Press 2013

First published 2002

Published by
E & E Russell
Beaury Creek Rd
Urbenville 2475
Australia
Illustrations by Pauline McCarthy

ISBN: 0958156301

© E & E Russell 2002

All rights reserved. No part of this publication may be reproduced, stored in a retrieval system or transmitted, in any form or by any means, electronic, mechanical, photocopying, recording or otherwise, without the prior written permission of the copyright owner.

REPRINTED BY PERMISSION
Copyright © 2013 by Xenophon Press LLC

Edited by Richard and Frances Williams

All rights reserved. No part of this work may be reproduced or transmitted in any form or by any means, electronic or mechanical, including photocopying, or by any information storage or retrieval system except by a written permission from the publisher.

Published by Xenophon Press LLC

7518 Bayside Road, Franktown, Virginia 23354-2106, U.S.A.

ISBN-10   933316372
ISBN-13   9780933316379

Cover design by Naia Poyer

Table of Contents

Acknowledgements	iii
Preface to the Xenophon Press Edition	iv
Introduction	2
Beginning Shoulder-in	11
Contra Shoulder-in	16
Spirals	18
Leg-yield	24
Shoulder-in	26
Serpentines	32
Warming-up	38
Loops	40
Corners	47
Circles	51
Straight Lines	53
Travers	55
Half-Pass	62
Renvers	68
Small Jumping and Cavalletti	71
Variations of Suppling exercises	77
Transitions	82

Contents continued

Halt	89
Walk—Canter—Walk	94
Contra Canter	97
Collection	102
Rein-Back	105
Pirouettes	107
Canter Pirouette	111
Extended Trot	115
Flying Changes	120
Tempi Changes	128
Piaffe and Passage	131

Acknowledgements

I have had a lot of help from friends whilst doing this book.

Venn & David who gave me the use of their house for quiet, but fed me so well I put on weight and who only stopped short of chaining me to the computer.

Diane, who had me as a guest while I was typesetting with Linda, who had to somehow put up with my pickiness on every detail.

To Fran who originally conned me into writing articles for Hoofs & Horns, *and who has continuously encouraged me!*

Pauline, whose imagination and initiative with the illustrations on numerous occasions saved my sanity.

To the great trainers I have been lucky enough to have had access to, and of course my wonderful horses who were just the best teachers.

And lastly my daughter who not only looked after home and farm, but who rode and trained my young horse while I was away, and now, she is far better than me.

Eleanor Russell

Preface to the Xenophon Press Edition

Eleanor Russell has a unique way of simplifying the gymnastic exercises and has a refreshingly positive approach to riding, patterning and problem solving that has helped countless riders and trainers all over the world. Her no frills, direct style along with her enthusiasm makes her recommendations very approachable by the beginner and advanced rider alike. Key to her successful approach is the self-examination process. After each of her exercises, she expects the rider to critically observe what exactly happened, to be open to unlimited success, to accept responsibility for struggles and temporary failure. Faced with failure or less than stellar results, she gives the rider encouragement as to what to try differently, what could have been the rider's error, and encouragement to try again.

Common to all of her correction recommendations is that the rider must never blame the horse. The rider is not 'to blame' *per se,* but is definitely responsible for making changes, revisions, and critical observations to their own potential flaws, errors or omissions.

This book is the next best thing to having a riding lesson from Eleanor Russell. We are grateful to Nadja King of *Horses for Life* magazine for introducing us to Eleanor's work and to her daughter, Emma, for facilitating this reprint edition.

The Xenophon Press edition is nearly identical to the Australian edition, with minor changes to format and size. It is printed in America, making this previously hard-to-find book available to a wider audience than the previous editions. Xenophon Press has put its resources towards making this and other important works readily available to the English reading world. We are committed to keeping important equestrian works in print in the English language and to bringing new works and translations to light for the benefit of our loyal readership.

Thank you Eleanor, Emma and you, the reader for your support and interest.

Richard and Frances Williams / Xenophon Press LLC

*The horse has 436 muscles in his body.
They are all interconnected and he uses a large proportion of these every time he moves.*

Introduction

The subtitle [Wow! It worked. Help! It didn't happen] may be catchy but the most important thing in training your horse is to remember that:

"Imagination is more important than genius"   A. Einstein

If you train your horse to understand your language, your aids, then he will do what you want when you ask for it and if you use your imagination to mix and match the exercises, you can develop your horse to his maximum physical and mental potential, i.e., fitness, suppleness and happy, relaxed obedience.

The 'spin off' to this is that such a horse should stay sounder and work for you for many years and be more pleasurable to ride.

To be supple and fit throughout his whole body it is necessary to understand that only working the cardiovascular system simply builds up the heart and lung fitness. Yes, you have a fitter horse, but you also need to have a more athletic horse that can use all his muscles whichever discipline you choose to specialize / compete in.

Put more simply—you never see a ballet dancer, a sprinter or a football player warm up with just a few sprints in a straight line. They stretch and bend and exercise in every direction to warm up their bodies, the whole of their bodies, all of their muscles, before asking for more difficult or major efforts.

It is the same for your horse's body.

First you must warm up his muscles; stretch and contract. Short muscles (tense horses have short muscles) cannot build up, only muscles that can lengthen and contract will strengthen and build up.

This means bending your horse's body and varying the length of stride in all your horse's gaits but remembering that the rhythm in each gait doesn't change. Not faster, not a fraction, just longer and shorter steps called more technically longitudinal and latitudinal suppling.

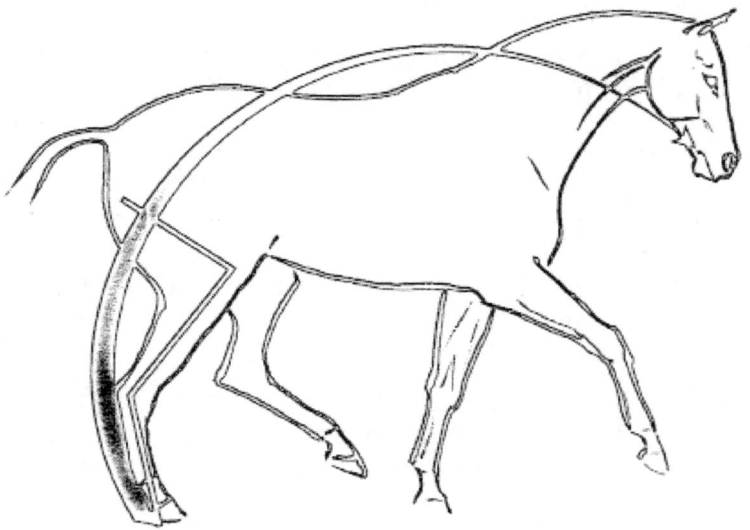

Create the energy in the hindquarters and then ride your horse from "the back to the front"

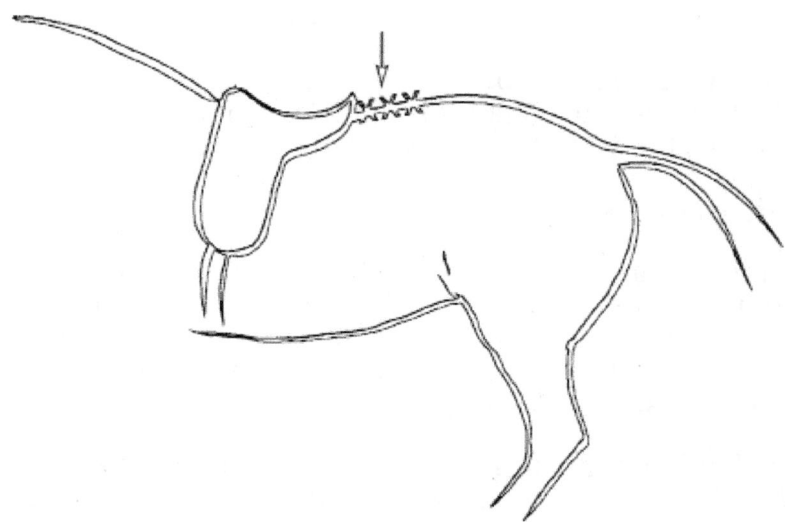

The spine of the horse will lift just behind the saddle so he can work with his back a little round.

The first time you begin to exercise particular muscles is when you change the diagonal that you 'sit on' in rising trot. Here you exercise one set of muscles, the ones connecting the diagonal pair of legs of the trot then the other pair when you, the rider, change and sit on the other diagonal pair of muscles.

So muscle systems (suppleness and strength) have to be worked as well as the cardiovascular system (fitness of the heart and lungs).

How can you do this?

Apply the normal classical principles of training a horse, and

"Build up your horse by simple exercises".   *Nuno Oliveira*

What does this mean? What sort of work?

Firstly you must understand about working a horse from the "hindquarters (the engine end) to the front"— as opposed to from the "front to the back" as many horses are incorrectly worked.

To achieve this, your horse needs to work in a round frame, the energy coming from his hindquarters and over his top line to relax the poll and lower jaw, to accept the bit.

Why?

Because to develop more power, he must have his hind legs under him to be able to engage his hindquarters. He can only engage (use more) his hindquarters if his back is round.

What does this mean?

It means that he lifts his spine 'a little' just behind the saddle so he can work in this round frame / shape. When he can do this he will be able to flex and relax all the muscles along his top line, his back will 'swing' (the back muscles will flex and relax) and he will relax at the poll and his lower jaw.

When this happens, to an onlooker his trot will become more rhythmic with slightly longer, NOT faster steps, and he will appear a little rounded or raised and supple in his back just behind the saddle.

To the rider he will FEEL more rhythmic in his trot and you will FEEL a slight 'rocking' in the trot if you do not rush but have this slow relaxed trot.

Remember, going fast is not going forward!!!

GOING FORWARD is, for me, a STATE OF MIND IN THE HORSE.

It is when he willingly accepts, without either physical or mental resistance, whatever you request him to do.

As an onlooker, look at the horse's face, look at the expression and you will clearly see a calm, intelligent acceptance of wishing to do what his rider asks.

You can see the horse concentrating on the rider's wishes.

That is the HARMONY of a horse going forward.

But at the moment, all you want to establish is a rhythmic soft trot that is incredibly regular. And it is this regularity, this rhythm, this tick, tick, tick, like a metronome that you are beginning to FEEL. Later RHYTHM plus ENERGY develops the natural cadence and expands all of your horse's movements within his rhythm and he can then move forward with impulsion.

He will also relax his under-neck muscles dramatically, where many horses have an unsightly, thick muscle.

When this thickness relaxes the onlooker can clearly see two lines appear under the neck either side of the horse's gullet. And the rider on top of the horse will see the muscles along the top half of the neck "flicker" and bulge out a little, as they begin to work.

Continued work over a period of time in this frame, lightly accepting the bit, in his own balance, will reduce and finally eliminate this unattractive underneath muscle and, at the same time, develop the top muscles and a more beautiful neck.

The correct way to develop this roundness is by first activating the hindquarters (starting the engine) and riding your horse from the hindquarters to the front.

Unsightly thick muscle under the neck

Soft and relaxed in the lower jaw and poll shows the two lines under the neck.

The other way is by forcing the horse's body into the frame that you want by the use of gadgets. Occasionally an experienced trainer will correctly, briefly, use a gadget. But 99 times out of 100 when using a gadget, the horse's front looks most attractive but his back is either flat or even hollow and consequently he is not using his hindquarters and not beginning to develop "engagement."

Confusing?   If he looks right, how do you know he's not right?

Try standing with your back hollow at the waist and then bring your bottom and knees forward.

You can't!

Now round your back a little (but keep your shoulders straight) and bring your pelvis and knees forward.

Now you can!

Alternatively, get down on your hands and knees and with a hollow back at your waist feel your tummy sagging down and you can't bring your knees forward. But if you round your back a little not only can you bring your knees forward, but you can also hold your tummy muscles up, as does your horse when using his back correctly.

IT IS THE SAME FOR THE HORSE

If the back is not a little round, he cannot engage his hindquarters.

Look at a friend's horse and see for yourself.

The other problem you could have if you use a gadget to obtain a round frame is that if you FORCE the horse into your desired frame/shape and CAUSE the horse PAIN in his body, he will very quickly find a way to EVADE that pain and develop a bad habit. Example: Hollowing his back more or coming behind the bit, which will be very difficult to fix.

How do you teach a horse to use his back correctly?

FIRST, teach your horse to react to your aids. For example, your inside leg.

WHY?

Because this is part of the language you will use to communicate with your horse and this language is called our "AIDS."

Is this the only language you can use with your horse?

NO.

By developing your FEEL you can read your horse's body language, e.g., you can watch his ears while you are riding him. Sometimes they are pricked. This is most attractive to an onlooker but they are pricked because he is looking at something and only part of his concentration is on you. But when he relaxes his ears, not pricked forward, not turned back, not moving excessively, but just softly relaxed, then he is concentrating on and listening to YOU.

We have all been told: your horse has to bend around your inside leg. Did you first teach your horse what you want? Or did you expect him to be psychic and to know?

Teaching the horse to move away from the inside leg teaches him to bend around your inside leg.

This is the beginning of you telling your horse to work from his back end first, and it is the first, simplest, but most important step to begin to supple his body.

But first you must sit straight in the saddle.

What does this mean?

It simply means that viewed from the front or from the side, you are straight and balanced.

How are you straight in the saddle?

Because there are many books available explaining the rider's position in detail, it is only described briefly here.

The most important thing about sitting straight on your horse is that you are relaxed with your weight down (like ballast) and that you are equal on both sides of the horse so that you don't unbalance him unnecessarily, that your heels are the lowest part of your body without being forced down, your hands are SYMPATHETIC and FRIENDLY and your presence has PRIDE.

It also means that in the effort of giving an aid you don't lean, or for example, unconsciously move your shoulders in reaction when you give a stronger leg aid, a kick, or even that you don't collapse in a hip.

Remember, you have hitched a ride on your horse's back and this effect is the same to him as if you were giving a friend a "piggy back" and YOUR passenger is not still or sitting straight, but moving around on your back and making you unsteady and unbalanced.

If you don't believe this, try and FEEL for yourself!

"POSITION" should always include RIDER ATTITUDE.

You should always be a friend to your horse, however firm you might be on occasions. Bullying your horse, or blaming bits and gadgets for a horse going badly is almost always only an EXCUSE for bad riding!

If, at any time you feel yourself huffing and puffing, or feel *agro* [to be angry or hostile for no reason] towards your horse, stop and walk for a few minutes on a long or loose rein and then begin again when you have both relaxed.

Ride like a king and your horse will carry you like a king.

Beginning shoulder-in

"Shoulder-in is the first and last lesson you give your horse."

François Robichon de La Guérinière

So how do you teach shoulder-in?

First by being simple, by explaining to your horse what your inside leg is doing and what you require him to do when you touch him with that inside leg.

How?

Begin by teaching him from the ground with a little turn on the forehand. Face your horse to a wall or a fence, and gently with the handle of your whip touch him just behind, but near the girth. If necessary help him with a very small vibration on the inside rein. If he steps one or two steps sideways with his hindquarters, STOP and PAT him.

If he doesn't, tap him again, and this time, reinforce it with a gentle tap of the whip on his quarters or just below his hip. He must take a step with his hind legs.

If he doesn't, be a little firmer with the whip, then AS SOON as he does take a step or two, reward him, pat him, make much of him. Begin again on the SAME side, with the lightest of taps and if necessary increase the tap until he takes 2 or 3 steps sideways with his hind legs. Repeat three or four times. When he has got the message, repeat on the other side. Keep rewarding him whenever he shows he's BEGINNING to understand what you want. Remember this is a new language your horse is learning!!

After a couple of days try it mounted, preferably with someone on the ground to help you if it doesn't work. Give your leg aid as a gentle squeeze then relax, follow with a small kick being careful ALWAYS not to bring your heel up and keeping your leg just behind the girth and relax. If nothing has happened, kick again and make a small tap with your whip on the hindquarters. Make much of him as soon as he takes one step and then repeat.

WOW! IT WORKED!

It felt like—You gave a small squeeze and relax, with your left leg and he calmly moved his hindquarters to the right two steps.

WONDERFUL! Reward him, pat him or stroke his neck gently! Speak a calm, soft word that you can always use so that he recognizes it whenever you reward him. A huge noisy slap on the neck or rump never seems to be a reward but more an advertisement to the world of how good the rider thinks he is!

HELP! IT DIDN'T HAPPEN!

* You gave him the aid but he stepped backward! You had too much contact. Try again with lighter hands, and try to adjust your hands so that he doesn't walk forwards or backwards. It's a bit like learning to use both the accelerator and the clutch in a car. You have to start on a hill without using a handbrake!!

* Nothing happened! You didn't squeeze and relax; give a small kick and relax, and follow up with a kick and a tap with the whip. First you have to start the engine!

* You didn't get it right! He just walked forward! You must keep the forehand still or nearly still. To do this, flex and relax your fingers - your rein aid. But don't jerk the bit in his mouth (very uncomfortable and unsettling to the horse) or resort to sawing!!

* It still didn't happen! Get a little help from someone on the ground who will gently tap the horse's hindquarters to reinforce your aid OR go back a step and get off and do it yourself from the ground again until HE understands.

You are finding it difficult. Well it's not easy to learn to coordinate all the aids and to remember to increase the aid if he doesn't react. Be positive and prepare in your head what you are going to do before you begin. Think it through several times so that you have in your mind exactly what you are going to do and the sequence you are going to do it in. But remember to stop before he gets bored or even begins to anticipate.

Remember

'A LITTLE WELL DONE IS WONDERFUL!'

A day or two later, advance to thinking first and then asking for the "turn on the forehand walking forward." Before you know it, you will be walking forward doing sideways and forward leg yielding: the beginnings of shoulder-fore or whatever you want to call it. Don't get too [preoccupied or] technical about how many tracks the steps are on.

REALIZE THE PRIORITY:

The important thing is that your horse moves away from your inside leg. This becomes an 8 to 10 meter circle with one step sideways, one step forward as you explain to your horse what you want.

WOW! YOU GOT IT RIGHT!

* He walked calmly forward a little sideways on an 8 to 10 meter circle, bending around your inside leg, coming against your outside rein as he bends, giving you perhaps your first FEEL of the connection between your inside leg and your outside rein. As he walks sideways forwards, it is a strange feeling as he seems to cave-in in his middle, each step a little sideways, as his back is exercised differently and he begins to relax. Be careful to maintain even / equal / regular steps.

If he tries to evade it by cantering or throwing his head up, "chucking a wobbly" [to have a fit of temper], etc., ignore this for the moment and achieve the important point—that he moves away from your aid, and therefore has accepted what you mean by the use of your inside leg.

Next time he won't be so stressed, he will accept the rider's inside leg—if he does trot or canter, it is a momentary evasion.

YOU have to be clear in your mind to be consistent.

When you start on the other side be super careful, use only the NEW inside leg and relax the new outside leg behind the girth in the correct position but inactive at this time. Allow your horse to learn one aid at a time.

As he bends he may relax in the jaw and drop his head. What are you going to do?

You are going to 'GIVE' as he gives.

'Give' means lighten the weight in the reins instantly (it doesn't mean abandon the reins and have a 15 cm (6") loop. He, himself, may also 'give' totally in the inside rein as he comes through laterally. Don't immediately take up a contact with that inside rein, leave it for the moment and FEEL the CONTACT on the OUTSIDE rein and WHAT A FEELING! You now have your horse between your inside leg and your outside rein.

HELP! IT DIDN'T HAPPEN!

* **He just walked straight on a small circle.** Go back to the first lesson, the turn on the forehand and make sure HE understands your inside leg. Then try one step sideways, one step forward, one step sideways, and so on. It is important that you achieve the sideways step from your leg and the horse should be bending away from your [inside] leg and not from your hands. Be especially sure

that you don't use the inside rein to obtain the [sideways movement; it should be a result of moving] away from the inside leg.

If you do it a bit too slowly but get it right WONDERFUL. Next time not only will it be easier, but more forward!

Keep a mental picture of the best sideways—forward on a small circle in your mind (even if it was on video). It will be a positive incentive and soon you will do it as well as in your mental picture.

Don't fall into the trap of trying to walk sideways by your hands if he doesn't react to your leg. Remember your priority is your leg aid. You have to start the engine first!

This reaction to your inside leg is the first lesson of what are called "the basics."

To again quote the 18th century master horse trainer, de la Guérinière.

"The first and last lessons are always shoulder-in."

And this is the beginning of shoulder-in.

Remember, as soon as you get a reaction away from your inside leg a step or two sideways...REWARD him! ...and RELAX the rein and a few steps forwards. Begin again but first, tell him he is wonderful! And gently scratch on the inside of his neck.

And when you repeat it, always start with the smallest aid, before using the bigger, stronger aid!

Here you have also begun to exercise and strengthen his hind legs one at a time. By moving the inside hind leg inward, underneath him, he begins to carry more weight on it and consequently builds up the strength and power in that leg and then in the other hind leg when you change direction.

It should always, always be MAXIMAL effort from the horse and MINIMAL effort from the rider.

As your aids become lighter until they are feather light, and your horse's reactions are instant, you will develop a fantastic RAPPORT with your FRIEND, your HORSE.

Next, you progress to the contra-shoulder-in [counter shoulder-in, or shoulder-out].

Contra Shoulder-in (sometimes called 'head to the wall.')

This next step, called the reverse or contra-shoulder-in, and sometimes when the angle gets a little bigger and you lose the bend in the horse's body, it becomes a reverse leg yield.

On the short side of the arena, walk on the RIGHT rein along the track. After the corner, take both hands a little to the LEFT and flex and relax your fingers to ask and keep your horse looking, flexed to the LEFT. And, at the same time, your left leg gives the aid for the horse to walk sideways (not more than a 30 degree angle to the wall) down the track/wall, with the quarters to the inside of the track, and your outside leg is relaxed, just behind the girth.

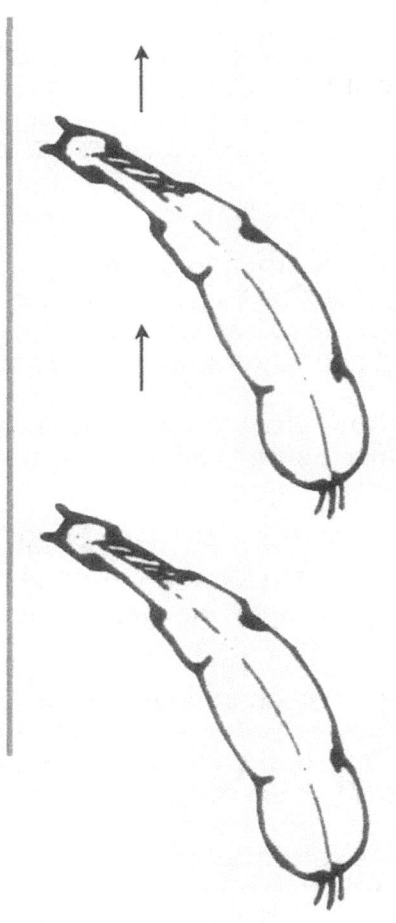

This is the same principle, same aids as before but often easier for a young horse along a wall, than to progress immediately to shoulder-in down the long side where the rider is tempted and frequently does resort to using too much hands, especially using the inside rein, which is incorrect.

How does it FEEL?

The horse is moving a little sideways down the track because his quarters are to the inside of the track, and he is bent around your LEFT [called the rider's 'inside'] (outside of the *manège*) leg.

Confusing?

Yes!

Your 'inside leg' is *always* the leg on the *inside* of the bend of the horse *regardless* of whether it is on the inside or the outside of the arena.

WOW! IT WORKED!!

* He stayed a little bent around your left leg looking to the outside and his quarters were a little in off the track but he FELT in his own balance.

HELP! IT DIDN'T HAPPEN!

* **He just stayed straight on the track!** Go back to the small circle and repeat the turn on the forehand / walking forward away from your left leg and imprint on YOUR mind what it FEELS like. Now repeat the same FEELING along the wall!

* **The angle became too big and you ended up halted at right angles to the wall!** THINK as you are doing all these aids and be aware of the angle becoming too big. You can open your right rein (take it to the right, away from his neck) and gently lead him the next few steps forwards down the track while giving little kicks with your left (inside) leg, without changing his flexion...He still needs to look a little to the LEFT. This will reduce the angle, and your priority remains that he moves away from your inside leg and continue stepping a little sideways down the track.

This is really quite difficult the first time you do it.

You have to ADJUST and REGULATE all these aids and sometimes you may get some strange FEEL.

For example, you can FEEL that your hands almost have a stop/go FEEL (this is not tight / loose) as you keep the horse looking to the outside but give to allow his shoulders to move down the track and then take / flex your fingers for a stride and again give a little to allow the next steps down the track. Sounds a bit complicated, and it is, but only to begin with!

This is why you have to be so clear about your aids and THINK it all through in your head at least two or three times before you begin.

Don't forget to repeat to the other side, we need an ambidextrous horse, not a horse that is one sided!

Spirals

This simple gymnastic exercise is so easy to do and benefits the horse both physically and mentally. With some horses, we do this before contra shoulder-in, and with others the head to the wall is easier, it is really up to the horse. The moving away from the rider's inside leg causes the horse to bend and stretch his body assisting in relaxing of his back just behind the saddle. And in rising trot, when he is soft in his back, it will begin to "swing". That is, flex and relax his back muscles as he relaxes into a more rhythmic trot, "gives" in the poll and lower jaw and his mouth becomes soft as he quietly savors the bit, producing a little soapy foam.

Begin at the walk just like in the diagram. It is just the same as turn on the forehand walking forward, a little more sideways.

Don't push, push, push with your inside leg, squeeze briefly and relax, followed by a little kick and tap with the whip if necessary. At the same moment flex your fingers to prevent too much forwards, then 'give' a little.

WOW!   YOU GOT IT RIGHT!

* How did it feel? The rider will feel the effort of the horse's sideways steps at walk as his body stretches and relaxes. Then at trot you will FEEL the more rhythmic steps as his back becomes softer to sit on and as he is 'THROUGH" in his body, the contact will be softer and especially on the inside rein. This again is where you begin to FEEL the contact on the outside rein. This is the rein which controls the shoulders, i.e., stops them falling out and controls the forward movement.

HELP! IT DOESN'T FEEL RIGHT

* **He really isn't moving out on the line off the spiral.** Go back to walk and reconfirm the aid of your inside leg. Your horse MUST step a little sideways away from your leg. Remember to flex your fingers for half a halt as you ask him to step sideways and then relax your fingers.

*   **He is not stepping away and I'm pushing as hard as I can.** An even and continuous pushing won't work! The horse just becomes numb and the rider becomes exhausted in the leg, and riders should not need huge leg muscles for a vice-like grip.

Why not? Especially when so many instructors say Push! Push! Push!

Can a horse feel a fly land on his side, on his skin?

YES!

So can he feel you squeeze and relax?

YES!

And if he doesn't react immediately give your small kick and relax. If he doesn't react immediately to this second aid, GET AFTER HIM! Big kick and a tap, not a tickle, with the whip, again remembering not to draw your heel up or move your leg too far backwards - it is kick just behind the girth.

HE HAS TO REACT! MOVE! IMMEDIATELY WHEN YOU ASK HIM!

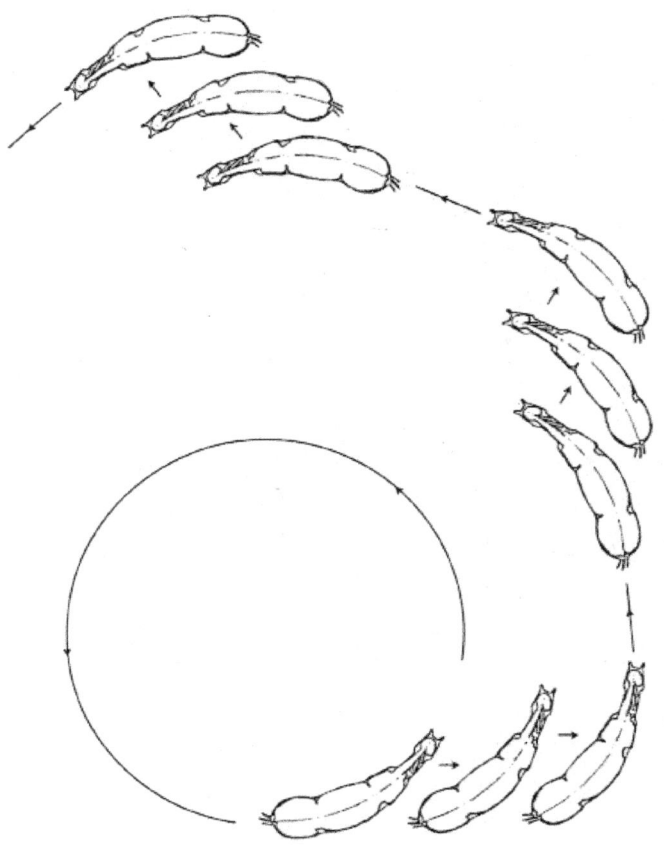

Move away from your inside leg for 2/3 steps then relax the rein for some steps forward and begin again.

19

If you don't think that this is important, not vital, at this early stage, think, imagine, how are you ever going to do tempi changes [in the canter] later? They can't be executed one or two strides after you give your aid. So you must be clear that you have to get it RIGHT NOW, at this early stage in your horse's training and then of course life will be a lot easier later because you won't be trying to fix simple basics at a higher level.

The same applies if you are aiming for a show jumping career. Your horse's reactions have to be instantaneous. Two or three strides later could be one or two strides after the take off point for your fence, and where would that leave you? Upside down in the middle of an obstacle with the rails on top of you!!!

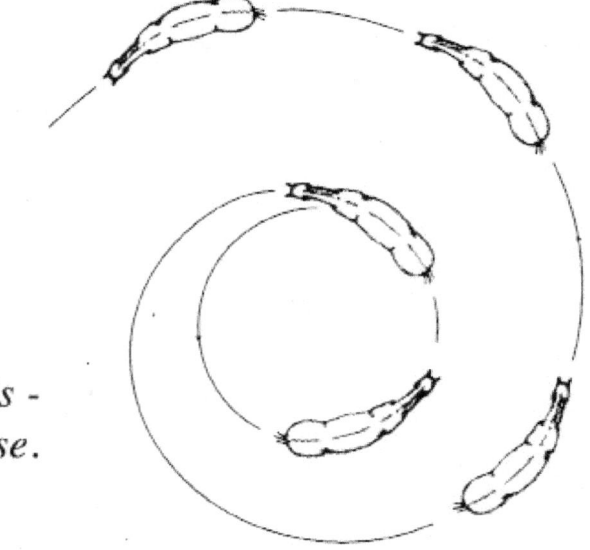

Variation on spirals - unwind a snailhouse.

An Obedience Exercise

The next step is to ride a little exercise for OBEDIENCE and SUPPLING and to see if you've got your AIDS CLEAR in YOUR head.

Ride a wavy line down the long side say 1 to 1.5 meters deep, that's about 3 to 4 steps [see diagram on the next page].

Come around the corner after the short side of the *manège* on the LEFT rein at walk and immediately see if you can ask your horse to bend away from your RIGHT leg.

He will bend to the RIGHT as shown in the diagram, and take a few steps sideways to the inside of the track and straight away reverse your aids and with the other, the LEFT leg in the inside leg position ask him to walk a few steps sideways back to the track bending in the other direction.

Repeat all the way down the long side, trying to get him to bend away from each leg with minimal use of your hands.

This will prove to you that your horse is accepting your leg aid.

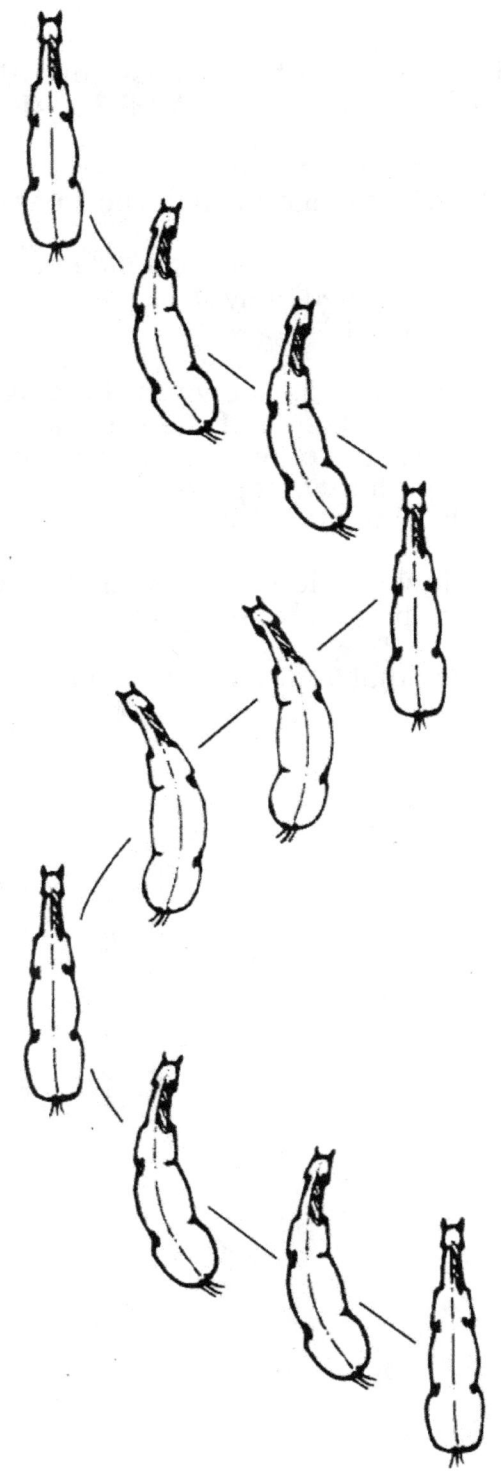

WOW! IT HAPPENED!

* It felt like a snake or slalom as he answered each new inside leg, one after the other, and even better you didn't force the bend with either inside rein.

Wonderful!!

You've taken the first step in avoiding the desease of *'inside reinitis.'*

WHAT IS THE DISEASE OF *'INSIDE REINITIS'*?

This occurs when a rider incorrectly uses the inside rein to:

* Pull the horse through the corners

* Tries to make the horse bend on the circle with it

* Begins and maintains the shoulder-in with it

* Makes the horse leg yield with it

* Stops the horse from falling in by pressing the inside rein

  against his neck

* And later begins half-pass by the inside rein alone

* And at a higher level you ruin your canter pirouettes!

Avoid like the plague, for all your life: the temptation to use the inside rein instead of your inside leg!

*Authors note: I read this wonderful expression some years ago and cannot find the quote again to give the original author credit, but it's not my expression; I wish it were!

Leg yield [this is the next exercise]

Start along the diagonal of the *manège*. This is not a gymnastic exercise but is a good obedience exercise for the horse mentally and a lot more difficult for the rider than you would think.

WHY?

Because of the temptation to use your hands too much.

WOW!! It FELT great....

* He moved rhythmically, softly, fluidly away from your inside leg. He stayed relaxed in the poll and calm in the mouth. It FEELS as if he drifted a little sideways as he went forward along the diagonal, and you weren't tempted to use your hands too much, because he is accepting your aids! WOW!!

HELP!! IT DIDN'T WORK

* **He didn't seem to go sideways much!** The rider didn't insist with the inside leg, just pushed and gave up, i.e., didn't squeeze and relax / kick and relax, and when there is no reaction you must immediately 'get after him'! Insist with a bigger kick reinforced with a clear tap of the whip. This may cause him to go sideways but he also speeds up and runs, once again you have to adjust your aids, take and give, with the rein to prevent the speeding up and maintain the same rhythmic walk or trot. Don't give in to the temptation to take and hold or you will stop the forwardness.

* **He stuck his head in the air!** You must have a stronger contact when he is resisting. You must resist, NOT pull back, when he is fixed in the lower jaw. You flex and relax your fingers to unlock the resistance and even more importantly you must "GIVE" in your contact the moment he 'gives.' But first don't forget to create more energy from behind to push him 'through' with seat and legs.

Again, by "GIVE" we mean lightening the weight you have in the reins. By making it more comfortable for the horse, he will realize he has done what you want. Relax, go forward a little, and ask again on the next diagonal.

Remember to keep telling him he is clever, he is wonderful.

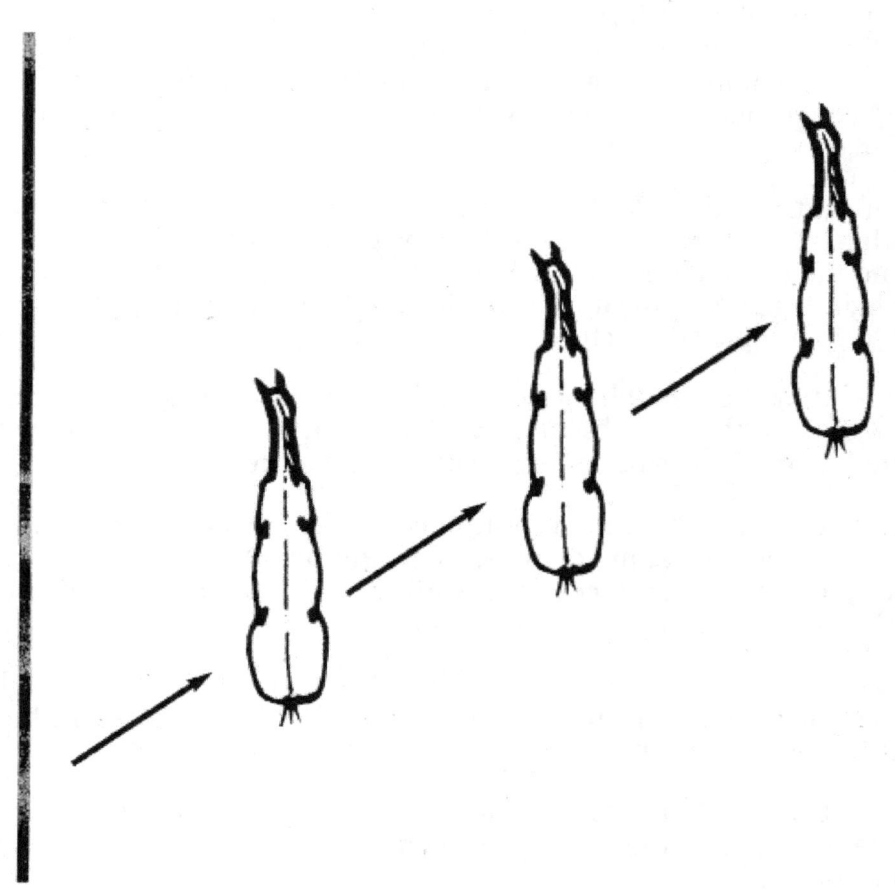

Shoulder-in

Many riders resort to immediately using their inside rein and hands to begin their shoulder-in, they take and hold and consequently block the movement.. AT WALK, commence in the corner just past C. Do a very small circle, two or more if necessary until your horse is light on the inside rein and then begin down the long side.

Bring both hands a little sideways to the inside, 'take and give.' You will, by your outside rein, bring the shoulders inward from the track then 'give' for a step to allow the horse to continue down the track. The inside rein only maintains the flexion, the inside leg says "continue down the track," while your outside leg relaxes behind the girth, and is there if you need it.

Repeat the little aids of your fingers / hands. Feels a bit odd to start with, but later when you have a really good connection between the inside leg and the outside rein, you will only need your back, outside rein and very light leg aids for a super shoulder-in. When you begin, you should have in your mind two pictures:

One is of the best shoulder-in you have ever seen, the horse is round, light, in his own balance, with his body bending around your inside leg like a banana, going forward down the track.

The second picture is not emphasized at this early stage much, but it is good to begin to think of it. Picture your horse's inside hind leg coming in underneath his body beginning to carry himself, which is the beginning of true collection.

Every time he begins to get the hang of it, gets it a little bit right, tell him he is brilliant and pat him. He will understand and have confidence to do more correct steps next time.

Two, three or four excellent steps can always be built into twenty excellent steps. Fifteen or twenty ordinary beginning steps will always be ordinary.

WOW! IT HAPPENED! It felt fantastic!!

* He seemed happy to go along the track with his shoulders just a little in off the track. He stayed round and your outside rein with a little take and give stopped his shoulders falling back onto the track. You finished with an 8 – 10 meter circle. This maintains the bend and he doesn't learn that he can go straight as soon as you have finished your steps. When you are confident that the horse understands, begin at a gentle trot.

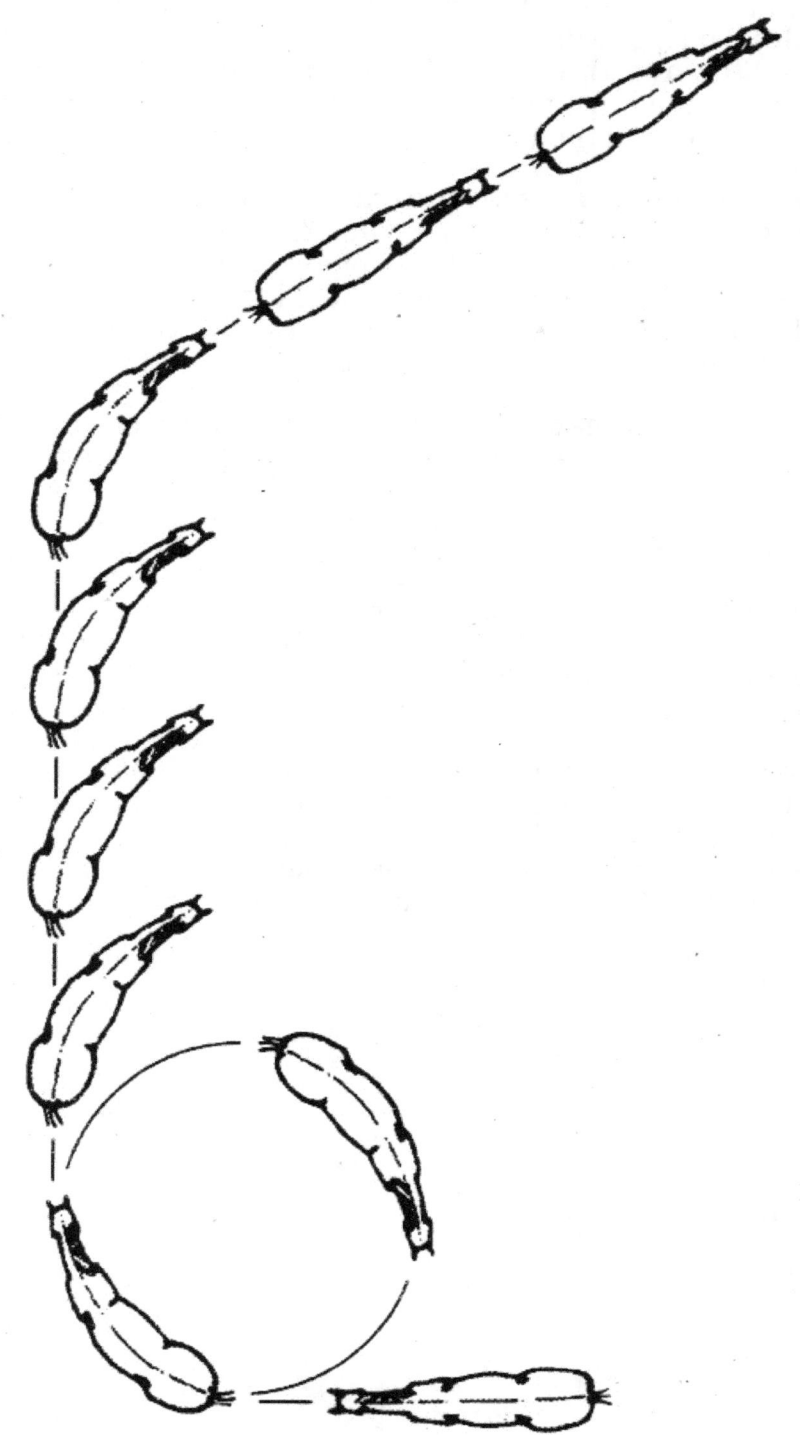

HELP! IT DIDN'T HAPPEN like that!

* **His head came in but he seemed to fall out with his outside shoulder.** You made the mistake of taking the inside rein and pulling his head in! **Stop and think.** Begin again thinking about using the outside rein to bring the outside shoulder in off the track. The inside rein only asks for flexion and then is light.

* **His forehand came off the track bet he kept going and walked across the arena!** Again this is you! You have to think through your aids, and give a little half-halt (flex your fingers, squeeze and relax) to keep his hindquarters on the track. These little flexions with your fingers should be enough to keep him on the track and you must remember to 'give' to allow him to continue down the track.

* **He tilted his head but the shoulder-in seemed good.** Your inside rein caused that. Remember more inside leg, less inside rein.

If it simply doesn't work and you are getting strong in your hands do this funny little version (see next diagram.)

Draw a line in the surface of the arena, a short 1 1/2 to 2 meters inside and parallel to the long side. This line represents a 6 foot high brick wall. Come around the corner on the track and do head to the wall along this brick wall.

When you feel comfortable at walk and your horse knows what you mean, take the next step and do your contra shoulder-fore at the trot. Make sure you don't ask for too many steps too early, or don't ask for too steep of an angle. Rising trot for a young horse is much better for his young back to come up and to round a little.

When you are confident with this funny exercise, do your shoulder-in. It is the same thing and because you have been doing it as contra shoulder-in along the brick wall you are not relying on your inside rein!

When you are sure of the shoulder-in at trot, try another variation.

Maintaining your shoulder-in, ask for a transition from walk to trot and back to walk.

You both got it right! Smile! You both deserve a pat on the back!!

HELP! IT DIDN'T WORK!

* He wouldn't go into the trot shoulder-in from walk shoulder-in. You didn't try hard enough to generate enough movement from behind.

* **You lost the sideways of the shoulder-in.** You probably asked too much with your hands and also actively used your outside leg. You forgot that the horse has to learn to maintain the shoulder-in away from your inside leg, your outside leg is relaxed behind the girth if you need it. You have to be careful not to activate any other aids when you don't need them.

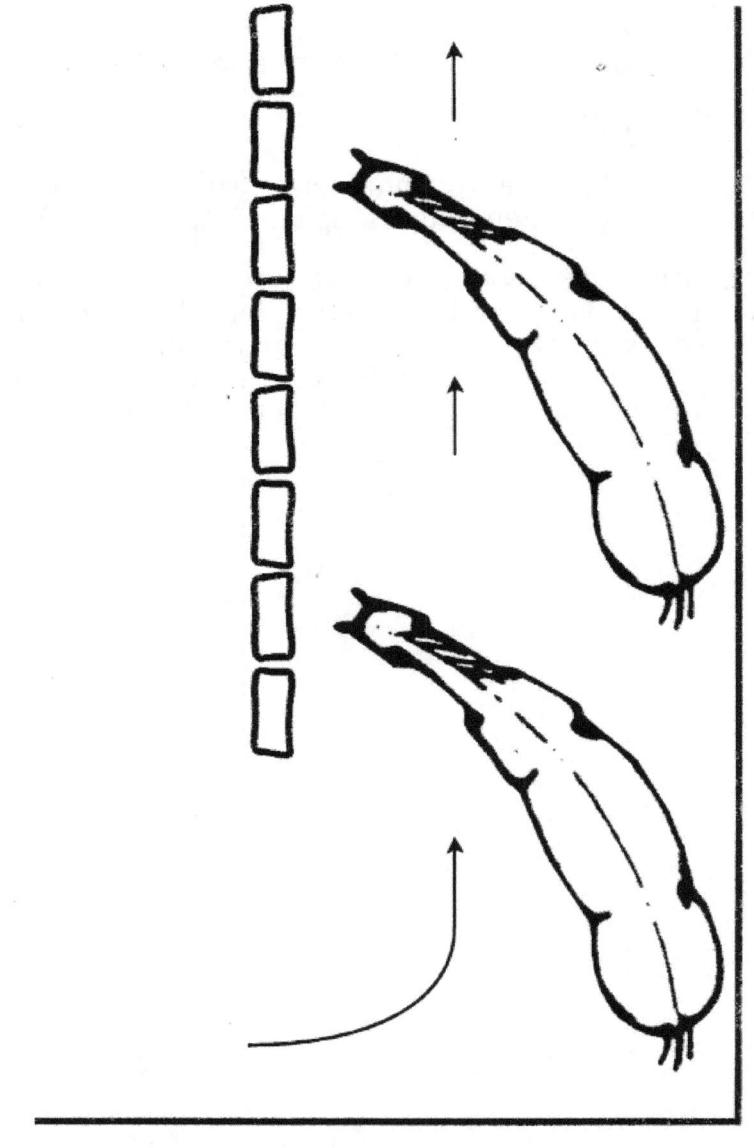

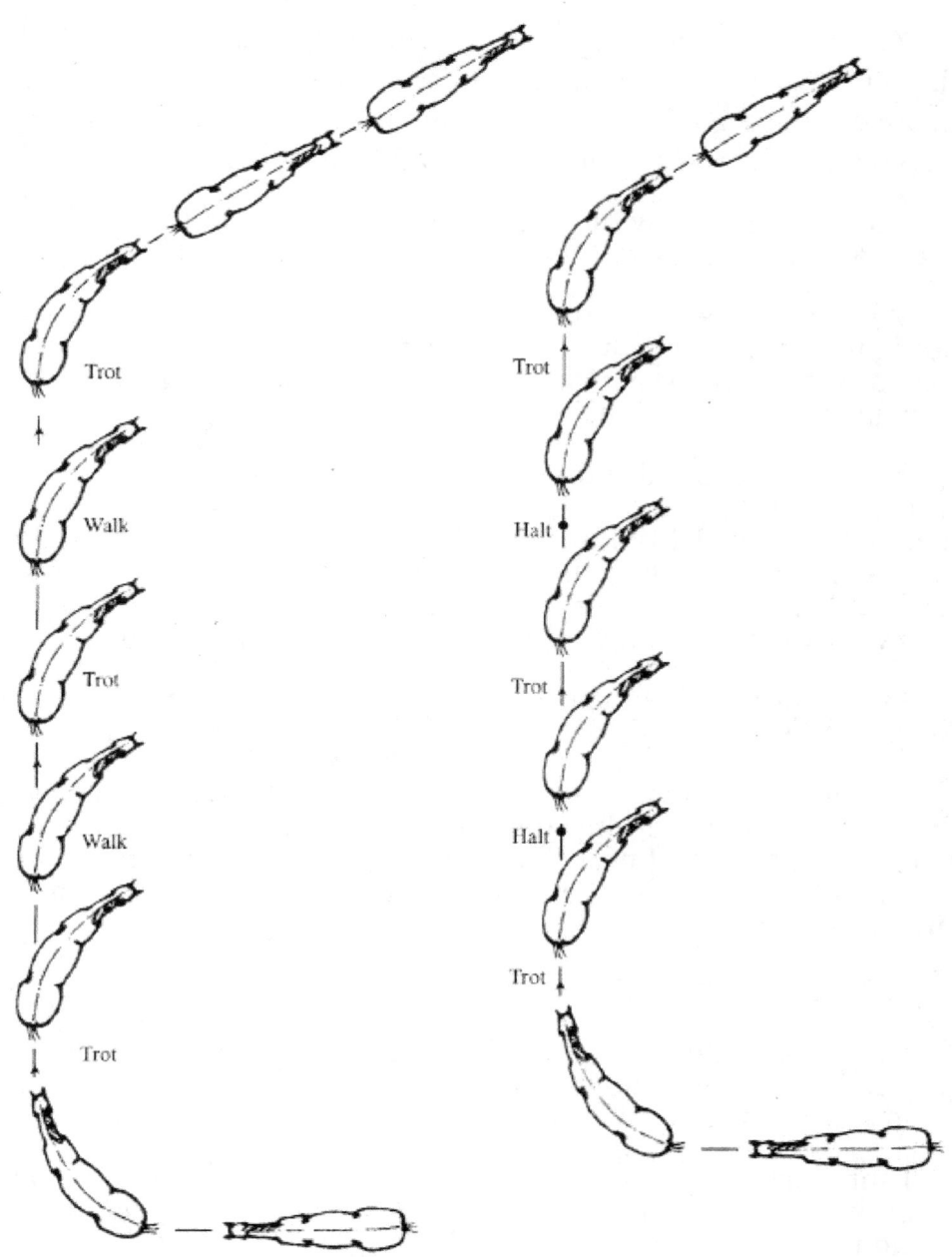

31

Serpentines

You have to understand that serpentines are a geometric fact of life. If necessary mark them with a line of markers out on the ground in your work area. You can use a tape measure for each half circle, also mark your center line and then add your quarter lines.

Now at walk follow the line of the first curve, but make sure you are nearly straight as you cross the quarter line.

Why? Because then your horse will cross the center line quite straight and "in his own balance." When he is like this, he has the best opportunity to change direction in a fluid, flowing line, staying straight on that line of the serpentine.

You need to break up [clearly distinguish each of] your aids in your mind so you can get the sequence right. As you cross the center line, your NEW inside leg activates the new inside hind leg and because your horse knows and understands about your inside leg he will bend a little and come against the new outside rein. This rein will control his shoulders and the forward movement.

Last, and hopefully least, is your new inside rein which is to keep him flexed a little to the inside, i.e., the line of the curve.

Continue around the curve and be nearly straight again as you cross the next quarter line and repeat the aids in that sequence as you cross the center line, NEW inside leg, new outside rein and last new inside rein. This sequence is, of course, quite quick so practice first at the walk.

WOW! IT HAPPENED!

* He flowed along the line of the serpentine and you could feel his reaction to your new inside leg as he immediately started to bend a little and placed his new inside hind leg under himself.

Fantastic! This is so important: he is beginning to learn to work from the back to the front by activating the inside hind leg, i.e., the hindquarters FIRST.

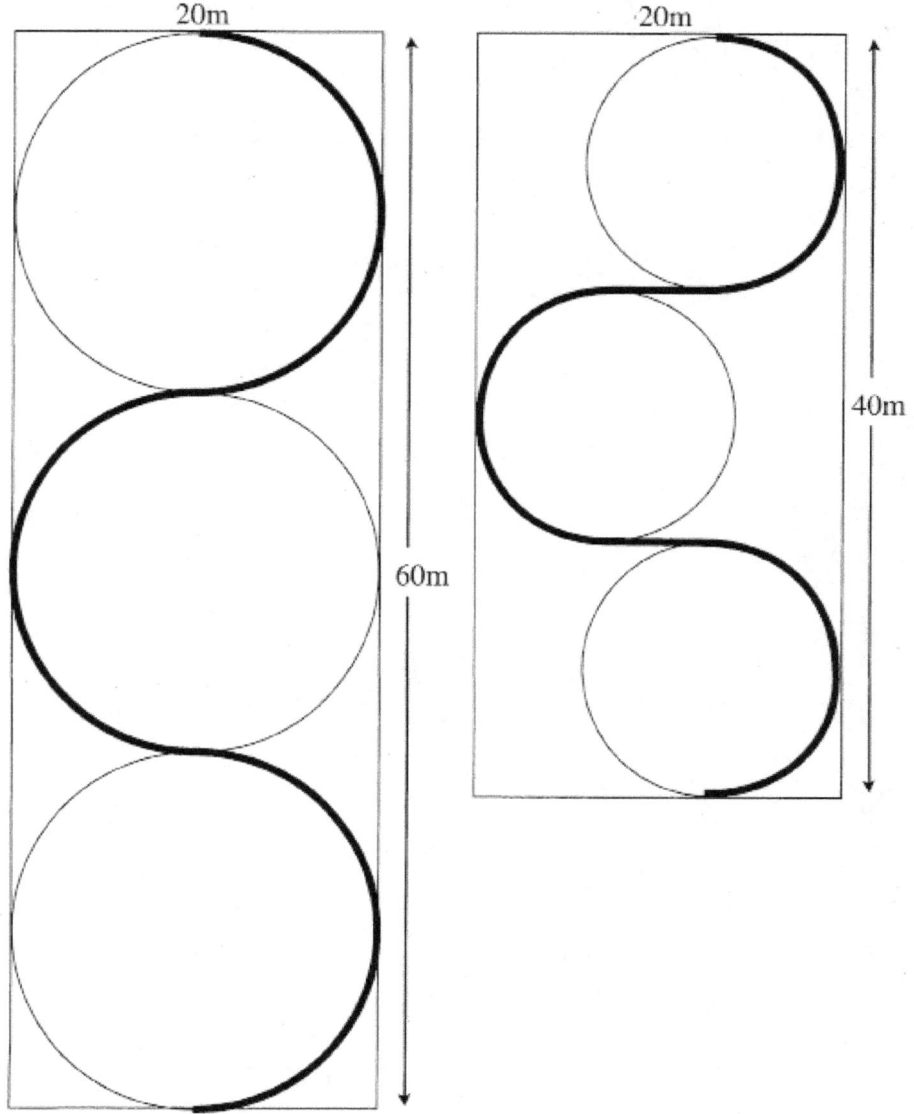

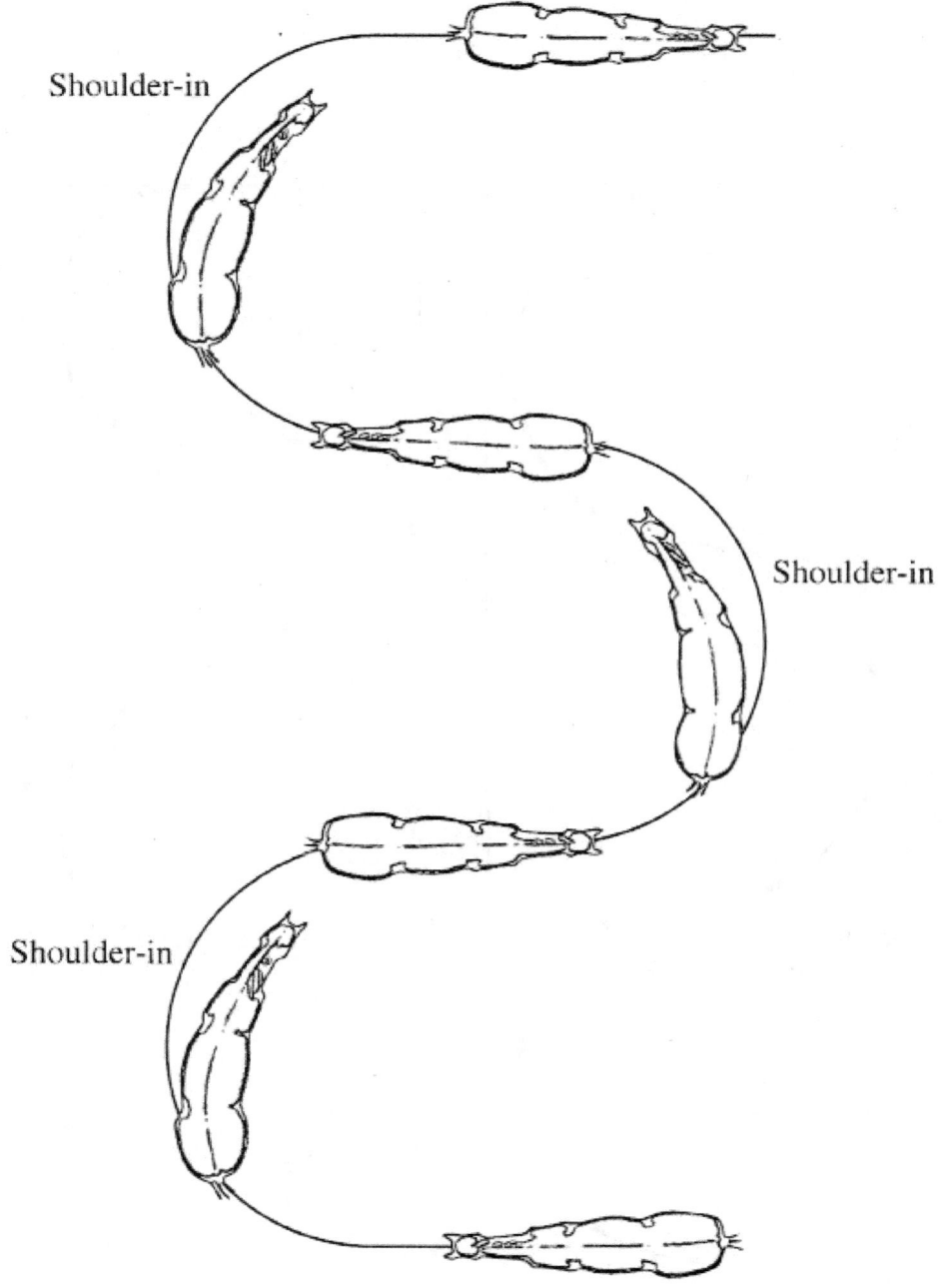

HELP! IT DIDN'T HAPPEN!

* I used my inside leg and he bent but he kept on bending and fell out, off the line. You forgot to stop using your inside leg and where was your outside rein? Remember to stop using your inside leg and straighten him with your outside rein but adjust / FEEL how much of an aid you need.

* He didn't bend and fell in with his inside shoulder. You must correct this immediately. Do a half-halt to get his attention and insist that he move / bend away from your inside leg as in the earlier exercise of one step sideways, one step forward. Don't expect the line to remain a good serpentine while doing this correction. The priorities are: he HAS to accept that inside leg and bend a little.

* He began to trot. He misinterpreted your aids. You must flex and relax your fingers a little to reduce his desire to trot, but give to allow him to still go forward while bending along the line.

Variations when riding a serpentine

Put a halt in each time you cross the center line, make sure you vary the time you stand still and sometimes pat your horse and sometimes all over [his body] while at halt before you move off again.

* Put 3 to 4 steps of a small shoulder-in inside each of the curves of the loops.

* Put a small circle inside each of the curves.

* Put it all together and mix up the shoulder-in steps, a small circle, some halts, etc. I.e., use your imagination.

The above can all be done at walk first and then at a relaxed calm trot, rise if you feel happier / more comfortable, especially for a young horse, remembering the priorities are rhythm, bend and correctness of your line.

Again you have to learn to adjust your aids. Don't use them all just because you know about them.

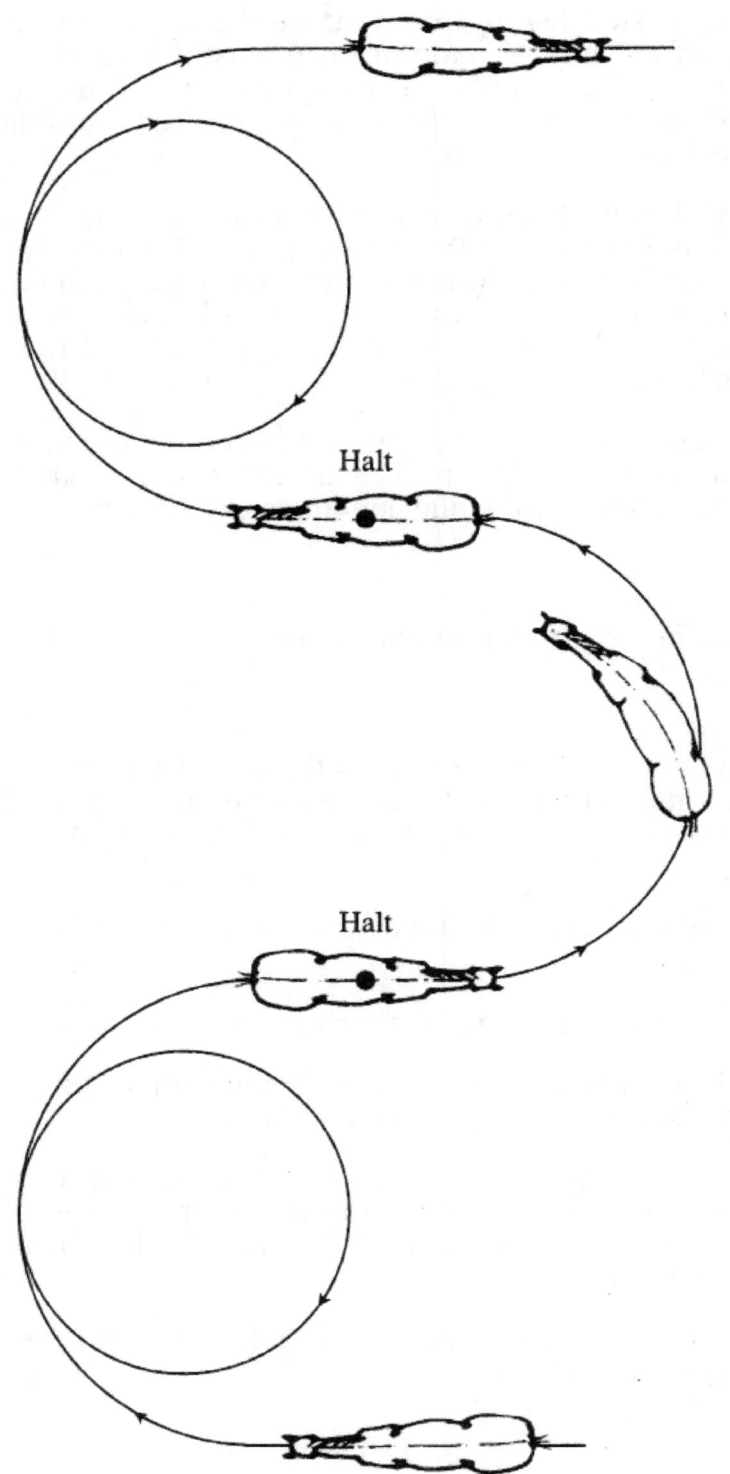

Here we are beginning to expand your horse's vocabulary, his physical suppleness and FLEXIBILITY. He is becoming relaxed in the poll and accepting the bit in a calm, soft way.

Your horse can now move away from each inside leg. He can bend 'laterally' (as it is called) in both directions. The way for him to become more supple, more FLEXIBLE in his body, is now established.

You are aiming for a happily obedient horse that is supple, ATHLETIC and can therefore perform the tasks that you ask more easily. And the spin off from this is that he has less chance of breaking down when you ask a big effort of him because his body is tuned, fit and supple, and consequently he should stay sound longer,

In these early days of training your horse, all this may not take you very long during your daily ride on your horse. So what else can you do to work your horse and benefit more parts of his body and muscles? You don't boringly go back to the same sitting trot in mind numbing 20 meter circles. Instead, think calmly about your horse's body and the previous exercises.

Can you vary them?

Apply them in different and more interesting ways as you ride your horse for approximately 45 minutes?

Flexibility of how you work and what you do should be in your mind all the time, every day. PREPARATION of what you want to do, work at, and achieve when riding your horse is VITAL; but even more important is that you remain FLEXIBLE in your mind as the work progresses.

All of this can vary depending on your horse's age and his general fitness etc. Some horses require less work, some a little more. Think about your horse's body and his mind as you work him. He is your friend, not a machine.

You have to use your imagination with the simple exercises, stretch your mind as you begin to develop a progression, a set of aerobics for your horse. Also, and most importantly, learn to FEEL how you should use these variations of the exercises.

Again remember Einstein: "imagination is more important than genius."

And also remember Nuno Oliveira: "you build up your horse with simple exercises."

The most important work you do with your horse each day is

your transitions and the variations of what you ask of your horse. The more changes of pace, i.e., length of stride within the same rhythm, the more transitions per ride the sooner your horse will become adept at reading your signals / aids and become obedient and supple.

WARMING UP

To begin with, walk on a long rein for some minutes after you get on your horse and then with a little shorter rein with a light contact, at a medium walk, still the same walk, same rhythm. Not collected walk!

Walk unwinding spirals in both directions, this gives your horse the chance for his body to loosen some muscles before you ask more. Think about any athlete, ballerina or gymnast. They all warm up their muscles slowly. Why not your horse? And don't forget he can't tell you [verbally] whether he is stiff or a little sore somewhere [in his body] (not lame) or even if he slept badly, so give his body a chance to loosen up.

Take some minutes at walk unwinding your spirals in each direction. Now trot your spirals, be sure he is reacting to the use of your inside leg, and you are not leading him out on the [spiral] line with your hands! Also be sure he is rhythmic and even in his steps and soft in the poll.

WOW! IT FELT SO GOOD!

* He is bending away from your inside leg and stepping evenly and rhythmically as he moves further from the center of the spiral. FANTASTIC!

HELP! IT IS ONLY SORT OF HAPPENING

* **He is bending sometimes, but he is also speeding up**. This is your problem; you have to coordinate / adjust your aids so as he moves away from your inside leg, and, at the same time, YOU have to remember your half-halt and insist that the rhythm is and remains constant.

* **He is stiff and wants to fall on his inside shoulder!** More little kicks with your inside leg, don't speed up and if it doesn't work then 'open' the outside rein and help him by leading him out. BUT remember the inside leg comes first, especially not putting your inside rein against his neck to get him to move out! If it still doesn't work, go back to your turn on the forehand walking forward and be sure your horse understands what your inside leg means.

These should be regular steps, forwards, and bending a little sideways. How are you going to vary it?

Think!

At a TROT, forwards / sideways, ask for a few steps, then WALK, and then return to a rhythmic relaxed TROT, all forwards and sideways and on the same line/track.

WOW! IT WORKED! It feels fantastic!

* He stayed calm, round and soft. His steps stayed even and rhythmic, and he was obedient to your aids. You are clearly doing something right! Give yourself a pat on the back!

HELP! IT DIDN'T HAPPEN!!

* **He dropped his head in the transition to walk and seemed to fall on his face.** You used your hands too much and not your back and seat. Sit down, make yourself heavy, and then flex your fingers, followed by both [of your] legs [used] together softly on the girth to keep the hindquarters coming under him.

* **He chucked his head up in the upward transition and hollowed his back.** You need more activity from the engine, the hindquarters, and then you can momentarily fix (*fix* means *resist*, it doesn't mean *pull back*) with your hands as you insist that he goes forward from behind and accepts the bit.

Later in his training, it is a little more difficult to go from walk shoulder-in to trot shoulder-in and back to walk shoulder-in because it is on a designated track. This is a very good exercise for the horse mentally and excellent for you because you simply have to be very clear in your aids.

ARE YOU REALLY CLEAR IN YOUR AIDS?

What is the most important thing about giving an aid?

YOU ALWAYS GIVE THE AID IN THE SAME PLACE

For example, don't have your inside leg sometimes near the girth and sometimes nearer the outside leg [behind the girth] position. You will confuse your horse and he will lose faith in your aids and become dull and dead [to the aids].

MAKE SURE YOU GET A REACTION TO YOUR AID

If nothing happens, repeat and reinforce the aid until you do get a reaction, but do it remaining calm as you insist. You will find this won't happen too often if you get your aids right, in the correct place, and always in the sequence of [progressively] a little stronger. Remember not to 'push, push, push' until you have no variation in the aid or, what you see many riders doing: flapping their legs rhythmically until his sides are numb and he ignores you.

Loops

Loops can be deceptive to the rider, they look easy but often you see a horse leg yielding back to the track. They are a good gymnastic exercise and a very good obedience exercise.

Bend through the corner and gently bend off the track looking ahead to the spot where the maximum depth of the loop is. Here the horse must be straight on the line of the loop, then bend around your inside leg to begin back to the track, again straight back to the track, bending onto the track and through the corner.

WOW! IT WORKED!

It felt like a flat serpentine and he was bending, then straight, then bending along the line of the loop.

HELP!

* **The first part was all right, but he seemed to leg yield back to the track.** You have to be clear with your aids and remember the straight bit has to be straight.

* **He did a sort off half-pass back to the track.** You had too much outside leg which was too far back on the horse in the straight bit of the loop.

* **His quarters were out at X**. Yes it can be difficult, but again your aids have to change quite often in the loop and again always the inside leg which is a little behind the girth.

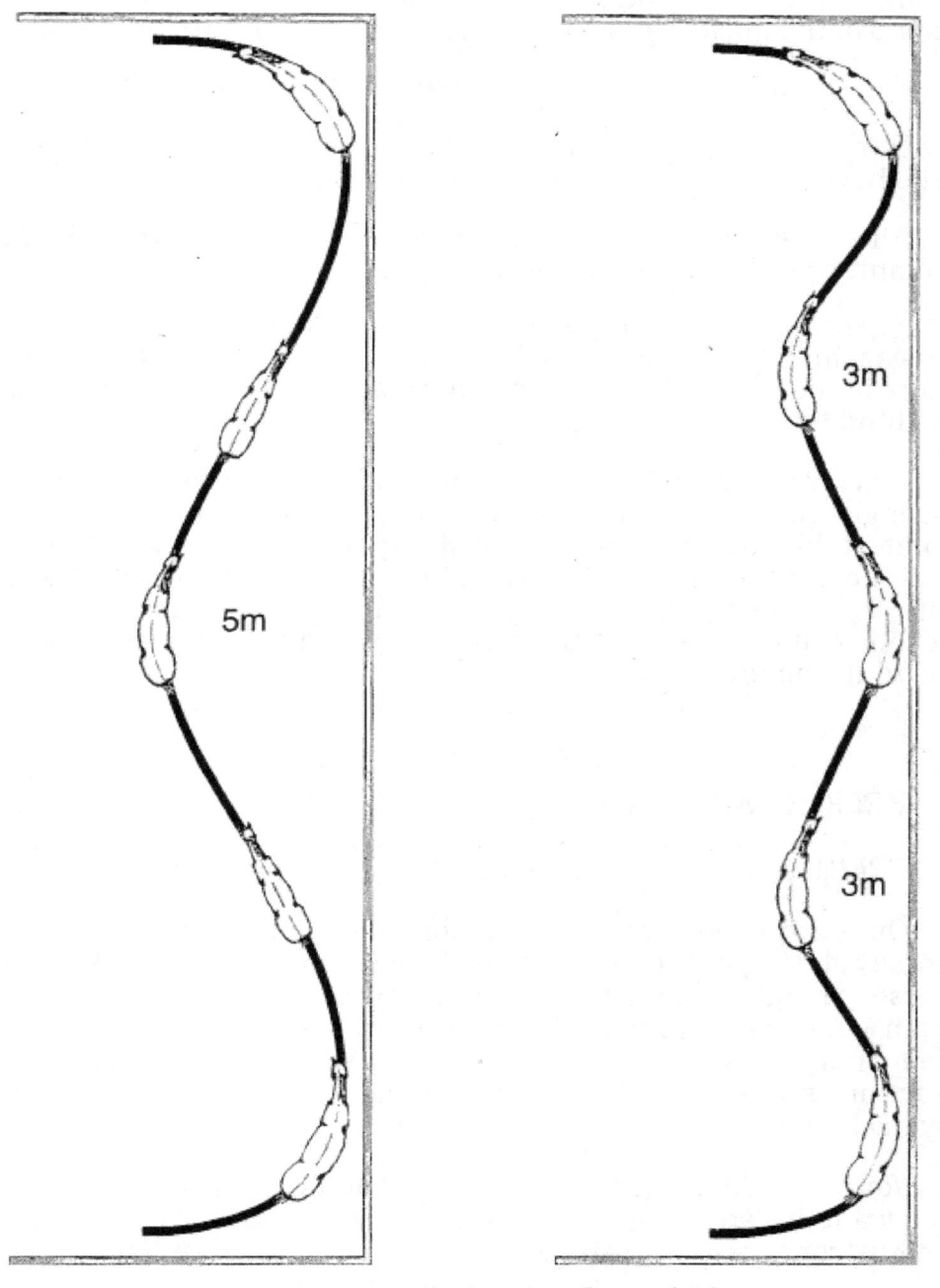

Loops are generally 1m, 3m, 5m and 10m.

The double loop

HELP !

* **You ran out of ground and couldn't fit it all in.** Don't panic, think about it and look at the diagrams. Preparation and looking ahead is one of the most important things you can do in riding a horse.

You should always look ahead between your horse's ears.

Horses are astonishingly logical and generally very obliging; it is us who have to be consistent with the aids we give.

All of this has probably taken up two thirds of your time. So you need to canter on both leading legs [leads].

Especially at this early stage, it is most important to encourage "engagement," i.e., the use of the hindquarters, by asking a little more in the canter than what he offers, and then he will have to use his hind legs.

It is far too easy to forget this and to slow the canter down thinking wrongly that a slow canter is a better canter, and especially if it is more comfortable to go slower! The most important thing about the canter is that the horse is straight, calm and that he stays round and goes forward into the canter *without* speeding up his trot and rushing so that he becomes unbalanced and then chucks his head into the air as he canters on with a hollow back!

HELP! HOW DO I AVOID THIS?

PREPARATION ~ mental preparation on your part.

On a 20 meter circle, first establish a calm, rhythmic trot with the horse relaxing in the poll and softly accepting the bit. Make sure your horse is bending along the line of the circle around your inside leg, not from your inside rein. Sit down—Sit in, feel both of your seat bones deeper in the saddle momentarily, and they seem to slide forward a fraction as you think: "The horse is going to canter from behind and not by my hands."

Your outside leg gently gives a clear and distinct tap at the moment you want the 'strike-off.' All your hands do is give half a halt if he speeds up his trot.

This may happen several times until you adjust your aids and your horse understands go forward into canter but don't go faster in the trot.

As soon as you've got your canter, the chances are it will be on the correct leading leg [lead] because of your insistence that the horse was bending around your inside leg.

Canter one or two circles and then [go large] around your work area, placing the emphasis on the quality, the jump, the roundness, the regularity, and the 'go forwardness' of the canter.

Round the corners of the arena so that you ride a large oval shape around your inside leg. It is more difficult on a younger horse to try to canter straight lines this early.

You can feel a bound, a small jump, in each stride. This is what you must have and must keep through all your work and try to improve.

HELP! IT DIDN'T HAPPEN!

* I couldn't get him onto the correct lead because he never canters on one of his leading legs. He wasn't really bending along the line of the 20 meter circle, so begin again but reduce the circle to 15 meters in diameter, or a little less, but remain calm, thinking about how you are going to ask for the canter. Remember your inside leg and ride around it as if it were an imaginary verandah post that you don't want to bang your knee on, so that the horse doesn't fall in on his inside shoulder!

If he does fall on his inside shoulder, forget about the canter strike-off for the moment and correct the bend, push him out on the circle several steps. It is the same FEEL as when you were doing the spiral, to get him to bend around your inside leg, i.e., soft on the inside rein.

When he's really COMMITTED to that BEND then, and only then, ask for the canter strike-off, but don't panic and use your hands, sit down, sit in, use your aids in the above sequence, and ask for the canter from the hindquarters.

Once you achieve your difficult strike-off, tell him he is a clever horse and keep going don't let him fall out of this canter. Being unused to cantering on this lead, he will be stiff and perhaps he'll find it not only unusual, but difficult because of the stiffness. So just continue cantering for several minutes without him falling out of it back to the trot, even if you have to kick him quite hard to maintain the canter.

The other reason [to maintain the difficult lead for a few minutes] is that this will exercise his muscles, and remind him that he has two canter leads with which to carry the rider. When you have finished, pat him a lot, give him a relaxing walk on the 'buckle of the rein' and don't do any more canter that day. This is easier than repeating the strike-off several times. It allows the horse to get used to cantering on this difficult lead before asking for too many correct strike-offs.

HELP! IT DIDN'T HAPPEN!

* **He still won't canter *on* the correct leg.** You will have to help him a little, add to the previous aids by opening the inside rein so that your inside hand moves right out past your knee and you lead him in the direction you want him to canter. Leading is not 'pulling back' it is leading him around gently and he will almost always strike-off on the correct leg. There is a [specific] moment when the horse's body is committed to the direction and he will always canter on that leg [correct lead] at that moment, the rider needs to learn to recognize this feeling.

* **He won't 'give,' and come light on the inside rein; while cantering on the circle, he keeps leaning on the bit and on the inside shoulder.** Gently bring him in on the circle, make it smaller and smaller till it's about 10 to 12 meters in diameter depending on the horse, and canter there, and he will give on the inside rein. Don't force him with your inside rein, take your inside hand out toward your knee and flexing your fingers lead him around the circle. As he bends, you must give with the inside rein; don't keep asking with the rein once he is giving and bending.

'Sit down' and 'sit in' is the same feel as pushing down on a swing.

This is a good exercise that also teaches the horse a little 'sit' as he has to begin to carry himself on his hindquarters.

After your canter work with a young horse especially, it is good to vary the length of stride at trot a little. With many horses you will find the canter work often improves the quality of their trot.

Shorten and lengthen, i.e., longer trot, short trot. At this stage it is only two, three to four steps 7-15 cm (3" - 6") longer because the most important thing is the rhythm.

This exercise keeps your horse thinking forward and obedient to your aids and especially reminds him to use his hind legs!

First make sure your horse is round, i.e., his back is round, because he can't lengthen if his head is in the air and his back is flat or hollow, then he will just run and not lengthen.

What is the most important thing?

That the rhythm remains the same. It must not speed up.

How do you do this?

You only ask for a LITTLE lengthening to start with, thinking and feeling with your whole body that the rhythm stays the same.

Difficult?

Yes, to start with. But think of a metronome on a piano and get the tick, tick, tick in your mind and FEEL your horse's footfalls / strides. Count or say a simple word over and over to yourself rhythmically until you become so aware of your horse's rhythm that you feel it in your whole body and it becomes automatic. So much so, that as soon as your horse's rhythm changes even a little, you will FEEL it.

To finish this working session, ask the horse to trot very SLOWLY on a long rein with his head down, not with his nose stuck out, but relaxed in the poll and round, on a very light contact. Some horses are happy to do this relaxing exercise at the beginning of their work. But with other horses you need to allow them to work a little before they are happy to relax. Be careful to keep your fingers closed on the reins in case your horse feels this is the opportunity for a playful buck!

You can do this! What did you FEEL?

Your horse FEELS astonishingly relaxed as he stretches all the muscles along his top line. At rising trot you will feel a rocking [motion], a hesitation, in each step as his back swings in this super relaxed, slow trot. Imagine you *are* your horse and try to FEEL the relaxation in his whole body.

After some days and once your horse has become accustomed to this relaxing exercise, you can bring it forward [earlier] in your work time. More importantly you can use it often during your work time to give his muscles a rest and a STRETCH. And later in his training, when you go to your first competition it is a great exercise to relax your horse when preparing for your test.

Corners

Now your horse understands and accepts your inside leg and this has given you the FEEL for the 'connection' between your inside leg and your outside rein.

Is this really important?

Yes, because this is the basic aid that you can now build onto.

Can you make use of this training / knowledge in a special place?

Yes, in a corner, a circle, a *volte* etc.

Corners are one of the first problems that you come up against when you first ride in a dressage arena. You are told that the track through a corner must be a quarter of a 10 meter diameter (or smaller) circle. But what do you do if your horse is not supple enough and falls in / leans on his inside shoulder if you try to maintain this particular track through the corner?

It is all a matter of PRIORITIES.

Is the exact quarter of a circle track the priority? Or is the horse bending correctly along a track through the corner the most important priority?

The *latter* of course!

If you can get it right with a slightly lesser bend, an easier track through the corner, it will not be long before you have it absolutely right in any corner, circle and *volte*.

The main reason a horse falls in or out of a corner is that the rider forgets the importance of the inside leg and outside rein, and also has not prepared ahead mentally for the corner. Before you begin any corner, circle or *volte*, think ahead as you approach it. Stretch down to the inside (don't lean), feel your inside seat bone and confirm the connection to the outside rein, [apply] a little half-halt if necessary and allow the horse to track through the corner without losing his bend or developing too much bend.

WOW! IT WORKED!

* You got it right. He tracked along the line of the circle, corner, or *volte* with a light inside rein, around your inside leg, calm rhythmic and soft. What does that mean? It means that both pairs of the horse's legs (front pair and back pair) are tracking with an equal distance each side of the curved track.

If you've got this good FEEL do it again IMMEDIATELY, and concentrate on remembering this FEEL and then get a bit adventurous and see if you can really 'give' the inside rein for a minute and then pick it up again, but keeping a light contact with the outside rein.

Now you have really felt your horse between your inside leg and your outside rein.

Believe it and have confidence in it!!

You are now well on your way with your basics and to getting high marks in your first dressage test!

HELP! IT DIDN'T HAPPEN!

* **How do you fix it when your horse falls in onto his inside shoulder in a corner?** Simply give a small half-halt and then correct him by asking one or two or three steps away from your inside leg, just the same as when you were unwinding your spiral!

Next time it may only take two steps to correct the falling in shoulder. Then the exciting time happens when you recognize the FEEL BEFORE he falls in and you are ready before it happens. Now you are recognizing and reading your horse's body language!

* **He had too much bend in the neck.** You took with your inside rein, because your inside leg was insufficient! If you pull back with your inside rein he has to give in his outside shoulder and it bulges out and he falls out.

Always remember, your inside rein has only one thing to do: that is to ask for the flexion and when you have that flexion it has nothing more to do.

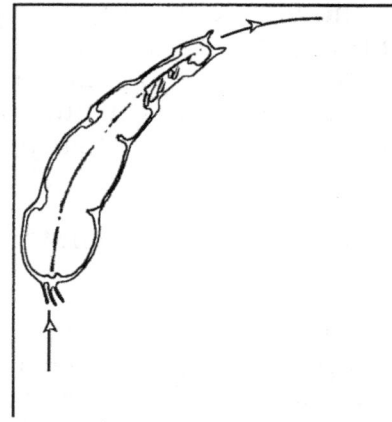

Correct

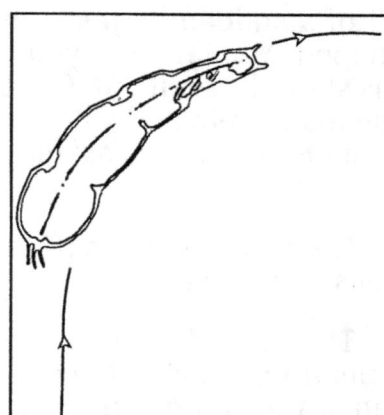

Quarters tracking [falling] out

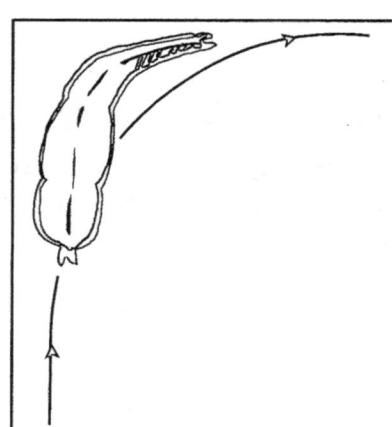

Falling out with the shoulder and too much bend in the neck

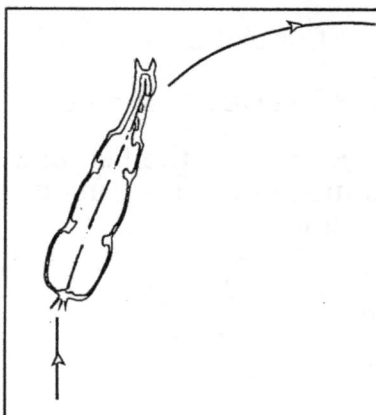

Incorrect bend, horse looking to the outside and consequently falling onto the inside shoulder

* **He drifted out on the corner, circle.** You had a nice bend through his whole body at the beginning of the corner, or circle, then all of a sudden he just drifted out and your curve became potato shaped! You let go of your outside rein (your guardian angel) and his shoulders fell out. Or you may also have taken / pulled back on the inside rein and without realizing it, given with the outside rein. Don't forget *to stop asking for bend if you already have the bend you need / want.*

Now your horse is beginning to be supple and understand your consistent aids.

This is really the beginning of using your outside rein to achieve something specific. Monsieur Jaap Pot [Dutch international dressage judge and authority] once referred to your outside rein and outside leg as your guardian angels, which seemed to be a really good expression to me.

Your outside rein is there, it may not be active at that particular moment but it's there to

* Prevent your horse's shoulders from falling out

* Act if your horse's shoulders drift out on the circle

* Control the forward movement

* To give a half-halt without losing your horse's straightness.

How does the last one happen? Your inside leg maintains the connection to the outside rein so that the horse stays straight on the line.

Circles

They are not as easy as you think. They are like serpentines, a fact of life. It was not until about 20 - 25 years ago, that I saw the cover of a book about by Harry Boldt [author of *The Dressage Horse/Das Dressur Pferde*] that it really hit me. On the cover was a picture of Harry Boldt riding a circle, a round circle with perhaps 30 photo frames of the circle shown in one picture. Every step that horse did on the circle was absolutely even in the bend and the flexion and they followed the line of the circle evenly. I couldn't believe that a rider could ride such a round circle. So, if you get the chance to look at the cover of the book. I still cannot ride a circle without that photo in my mind.

How do you get your circle that round?

We place pairs of empty 20 liter (5 Gallon) drums either side of the line of a measured circle, the drums about 0.5 meters to 0.75 meters (18 inches to 24 inches) apart. This depends on the experience of the rider including children who can have great fun doing this exercise. Witches' hats [traffic cones] with their sloping angle make the challenge too easy.

At walk, and later trot start with a 20 or 15 meter diameter circle with 1 pair of drums at each quarter hour [four 'points' of the circle].

Remember you must ride around your inside leg as if it is a verandah post, and your outside rein controls the shoulders, the outside leg is relaxed behind the girth (your guardian angel) ready to use if the quarters drift out.

Each quarter of the circle must be the same as the previous one. Some people ride the quarters unequally, i.e., with a flat / straight quarter followed by a bulge out that becomes almost a right angle turn. If you can't manage, put more pairs of drums either side of the line, this will force you to stay on the line and ride a very round circle.

Play a game with yourself, if your horse touches a drum, you are fined 20 cents, if you knock it over it's a dollar!

What does it feel like when you get it right?

The circle will feel astonishingly round, it seems your horse is turning a little all the time and evenly.

You can come down to 10 meter circles at walk and trot if your horse is supple enough, but at canter 20 meter circles are better to begin with.

There is a small trick to it. Look ahead to the next pair of drums, don't look down. As soon as you are lined up on the next pair of drums, look ahead to the next pair and ride forward, the same slow rhythmic movement and you will feel your horse is forward!

SMALL CIRCLES EXERCISE FOR SUPPLENESS

Begin at the walk on a 20 meter circle. At about C add a very small circle about 6 meters in diameter inside [and tangent to] the big circle. Do this by LEADING your horse around the very small circle by opening the inside rein out towards your [inside] knee and flexing your fingers. You will be surprised how easily he will then turn around your inside leg on this very small circle.

Next add an equally small circle to the outside of the big circle [on the open side] again about 6 meters in diameter

Once you are sure of the exercise at the walk, progress to do it at the trot on a 20 meter circle. After approximately 4 - 6 circles in each direction at trot, you will be surprised at how much more supple your horse is.

This is a very good exercise for very stiff horses.

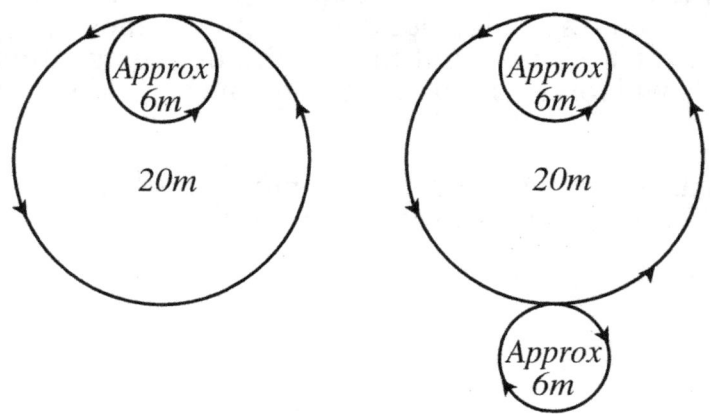

Straight lines

Straightness is very important.

Without your horse being able to be quite straight, you cannot progress to correct collection.

Begin developing your horse's straightness an easy way.

Don't begin riding shoulder-fore the whole [length] of the long side; instead just enlarge your 20 meter circle to become an oval. Then, when you can keep your horse straight on short straight pieces, make them longer until you can sustain this all the way down the long side.

It's a matter of one step at a time. You cannot go from kindergarten to doing your Ph.D. the next day! Doing it progressively, building one step at a time gives you the chance to check on yourself. You can make sure you are not resorting to hands first in your desire to force the horse to do it all quicker— even immediately. !

Riding center lines and other tracks that are not on the normal track against a wall shows you how difficult it is to be straight. Without the security of the wall, you have to be straight on your line.

HELP!

I can't keep my centerline straight when I begin a test.

Shorten your trot steps just before the entrance to a short, collected trot keeping your horse's rhythm constant and allow him to lengthen his steps a little then a little more as you go along the centerline.

By doing this you are riding him forward and the line will stay straight. Be careful the rhythm [tempo] doesn't quicken, the steps become longer, not faster and begin to collect a little before the halt and salute so the transition is not abrupt.

The entrance for a horse at collected canter can be very difficult if your horse has easy flying changes. There is nothing more embarrassing than 3-5 flying changes that you didn't ask for on the center line as you enter.

WOW! YOU GOT IT RIGHT!

* He cantered into the arena, straight toward the judge at C, you carefully shortened / collected the canter more as you prepared for the halt and he calmly halted in 1-2 strides quite square and there he stood immobile at attention.

HELP! IT DIDN'T HAPPEN!

* **He changed legs [leads]!** You didn't have your outside leg behind the girth very gently confirming the canter lead. Also take care with your rein aids that you don't give him a suggestion you want a change of flexion [bend].

* **He wobbled off the line.** You must have the courage to ride forward right toward the C judge. His straightness is the same as in the contra canter exercise on page 101. His shoulders must be in front of the hindquarters, riding fractionally the position of shoulder-fore even if you feel you are riding 1 to 3 degree shoulder-in, he will be straight.

* **He was crooked with his "quarters-in," almost curled around your inside leg.** You were using your outside leg too much and he was obediently moving his quarters in! By now he is competent and obedient at half-pass. You have to be careful and adjust your aids.

Now you know how you keep your horse straight on that wobbly center line and how to avoid the judge's comments of "quarters-in down the long side" especially at medium and extended canter.

HELP! IT DIDN'T WORK!

* **You were cantering an oval and he fell in too much, he didn't stay straight!** What do you do? You immediately stop trying to keep him straight and go back to the curved line and ask him to bend along the line. Why? This reminds your horse to respect your inside leg / outside rein connection and you can then ask again for a short straight line.

Ultimately your horse is straight when his front pair of legs and his back pair of legs are equally the same distance on either side of the straight line.

Travers or hindquarters-in

Travers completes your horse's vocabulary for his lateral work.

When you achieve this, you can 'mix and match' travers and renvers and later, half-pass.

In all of these movements, the quality of what you do is directly dependent on the quality of your shoulder-in!

How can that be?

Because the better the bend in the shoulder-in, the better the half-pass. There are two main problems you need to think about before you begin:

1. If your inside leg does not obtain and maintain the bend you will be tempted to pull back on your inside rein. This of course, will restrict or block the horse's forward movement, i.e., his inside shoulder and consequently restrict the inside hind leg coming forward under the horse.

2. The next problem will occur later in your horse's training. Now your horse knows and accepts your aid with your outside leg. So next time you do medium or extended canter down the long side of the arena and the judge writes on your dressage sheet 'quarters-in' realize it is your fault! You have kicked your horse with your outside leg behind the girth as an aid for lengthening and your horse has obediently moved his quarters in!! Correct YOUR aid.

The other problem that arises in beginning hindquarters-in is that in the rider's frustration they:

1. Take and hold with a dead pull on the inside rein. If you do this and can't get out of this habit, later your half-pass will lose the cadence and go into the ground.

2. The rider starts to twist in his body to try to force the hindquarters-in, resulting in collapsing of his 'outside hip'.

So teach your horse 'quarters-in' correctly.

Begin with your whip on the outside at about hip height. Be careful not to have it so low as to tickle your horse in his flank giving him an excuse to pigroot [A conflict behavior involving lowering the head and arching of the back and a kick out or bounding of the back legs (a minor form of bucking) often as a prelude to bucking].

In the corner before the long side at walk, ask your horse for a very small circle about 6 meters in diameter, bend him as much as you can around your inside leg keeping your inside leg against the girth, bending his whole body not just his neck and just before you complete the circle and begin down the long side, ask for his quarters to 'cut the corner.'

To do this, add you outside leg behind the girth and the same applies:

* Squeeze and relax

* Quickly follow with kick and relax

* And then insist just as quickly with a clear kick backed up with a tap from your whip.

Be careful that your leg is not so far back that it is in his flank; don't raise your heel even though your leg is back in the outside leg position!

Secondly again be very, very quick to reward even one step, just a GLIMMER of him getting it right.

This lesson is all a bit more difficult for your horse.

Why?

Because one [of your] legs is saying 'bend one way' and your other leg is saying 'move the other way.' So when he gets just one step, even a little step correct, you must give him a pat and tell him he's wonderful and very clever to understand your language.

WOW! IT WORKED!

* You FELT it when his inside hip came up a little under your inside seat as he brought his inside hind leg in for a step or two. Stop and give him and yourself a pat on the back and begin again.

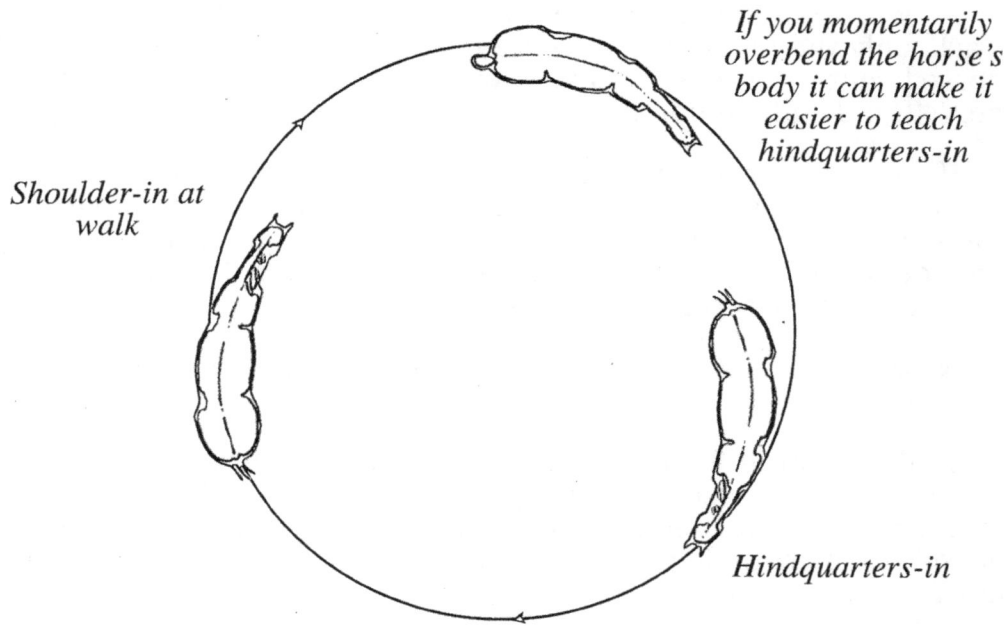

Shoulder-in at walk

If you momentarily overbend the horse's body it can make it easier to teach hindquarters-in

Hindquarters-in

Do it again and here you must be careful to ask in exactly the same way. So what do you do?

You think it through in your head each time before you do it.

PREPARATION!

It is vitally important and something experienced riders always do even if what they are doing looks easy.

HELP! IT DIDN'T HAPPEN!

* He cow kicked and didn't move away from the aid. You let your leg go too far back or your whip dropped and you tickled him in his flank!

* He moved his quarters in but lost his bend and flexion and the whole horse moved in the wrong bend away from the outside leg. You probably forgot to keep your inside leg very close to the girth. This time, keep it closer to the girth and insist, even if you turn your spur in for a MOMENT. Remember to adjust and use both of your leg aids, while your inside rein ONLY asks for the flexion and your outside rein allows your horse to go forward down the long side as he looks straight down the track.

As with shoulder-in, where only the shoulder comes in off the track, only the hindquarters come in off the track, the rest of the horse [front] proceeds straight down the track with the rest of the horse [hind end] behind him.

If it doesn't work, try hindquarters-in on a 10 meter circle. The circle helps the bend of the horse. Do a few steps of shoulder-in, even over-bend the horse (while you are teaching him) until he is light on the inside rein, and then ask for quarters-in, for one or two steps to begin with, reward him straight away.

Now you can do more exercises using all of these different movements.

You've laid the foundation for doing lots of different exercises correctly. If you use your imagination and vary the different exercises, combine 3 or 4 together, not only will you build up your horse's strength and power, but all of your working session will be much more interesting.

If it's not all happening, go back one step and try the following exercise. This exercise is good to do down the front driveway if you live in the country, otherwise in the *manège* from the long side to and from the quarter line.

At walk, counter shoulder-in away from the inside, right, leg, away from the right side of the drive (arena) with as much bend in the whole body as you can (not just the neck) or you will lose the bend when you add your outside leg, and this way you should have enough bend remaining for a horse learning the exercise.

If you end up with someone saying you have too much bend in the body, that's easily fixed, it's not having enough bend that is difficult to fix.

On arriving at the quarter line, or the other side of your driveway, do not change the aids but just add the outside leg behind the girth with little touches push the hindquarters across, and so half-pass back to the beginning side of the drive, or original long side of the arena. Relax the outside leg and with the inside leg repeat the beginning of the exercise.

When you get it right (it may take some practice) your half-pass back to the track will feel so easy as your horse does it in his own balance bending around your inside leg with the outside rein controlling the shoulders.

This confirms the aids to both horse and rider, and helps you understand the quotation "When you understand that the inside leg improves the half-pass you begin to understand."

This was easier for this horse than that horse; horses are all different.

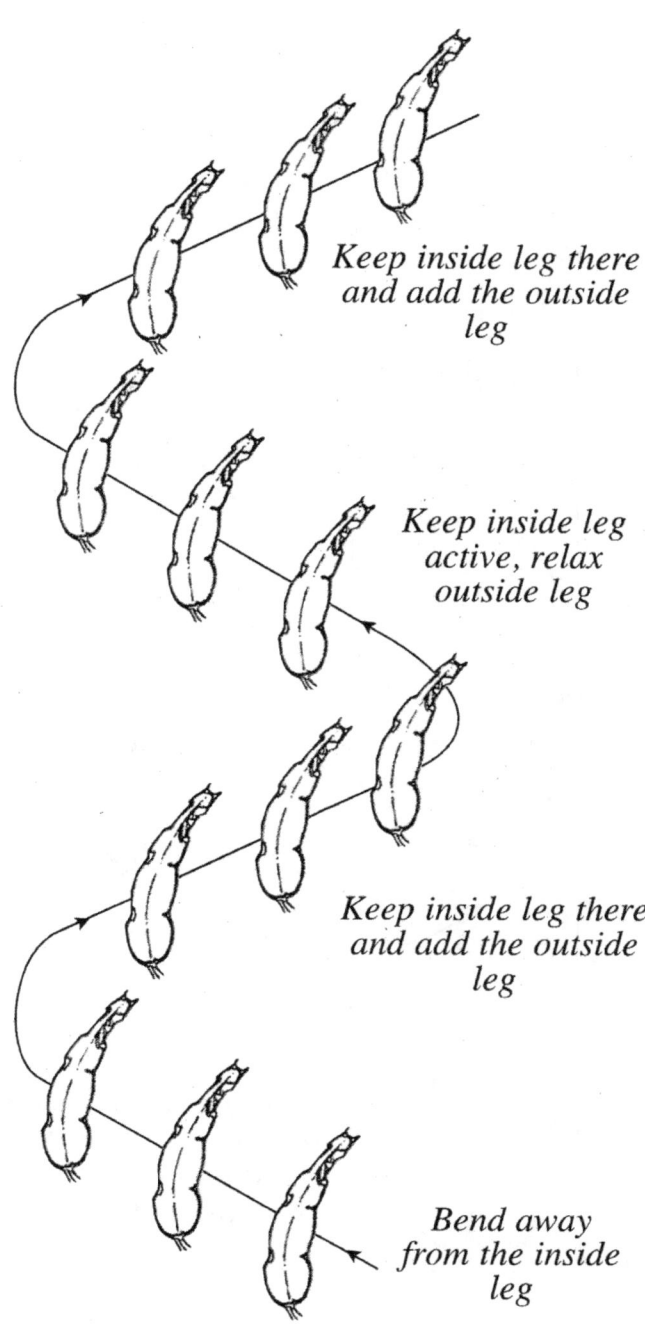

When the horse can cope with this in a relaxed and happy way, begin the following exercises first at a walk, and later progressing to doing them at the trot.

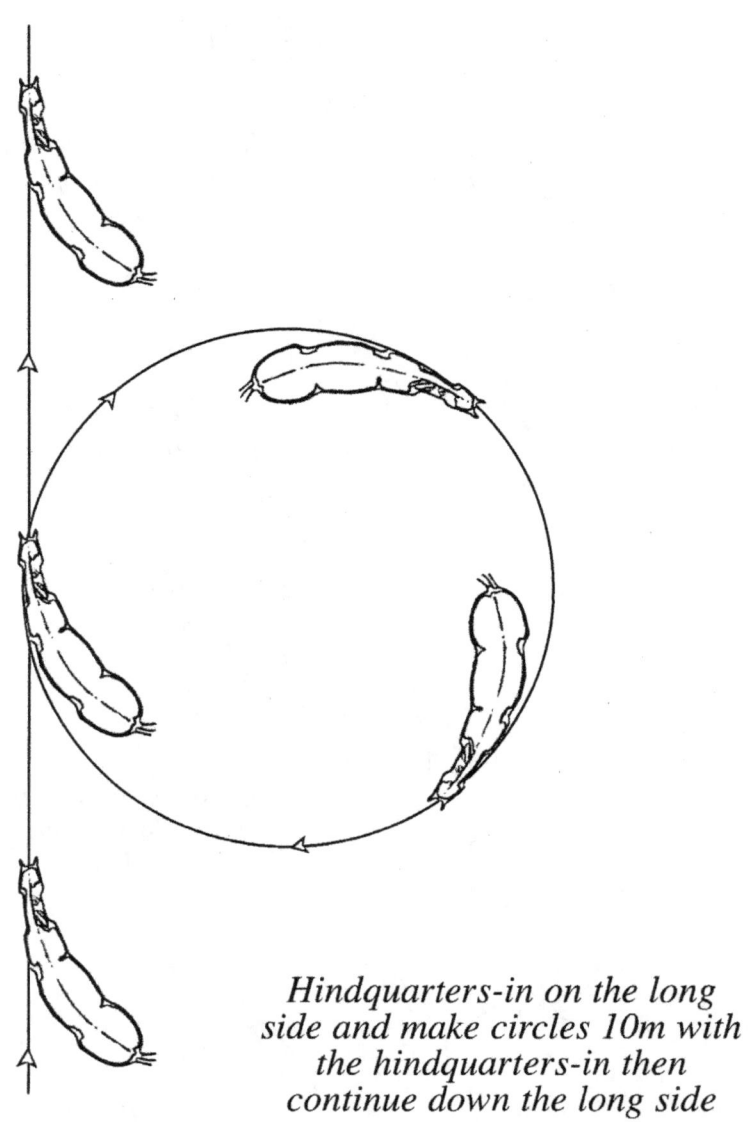

Hindquarters-in on the long side and make circles 10m with the hindquarters-in then continue down the long side

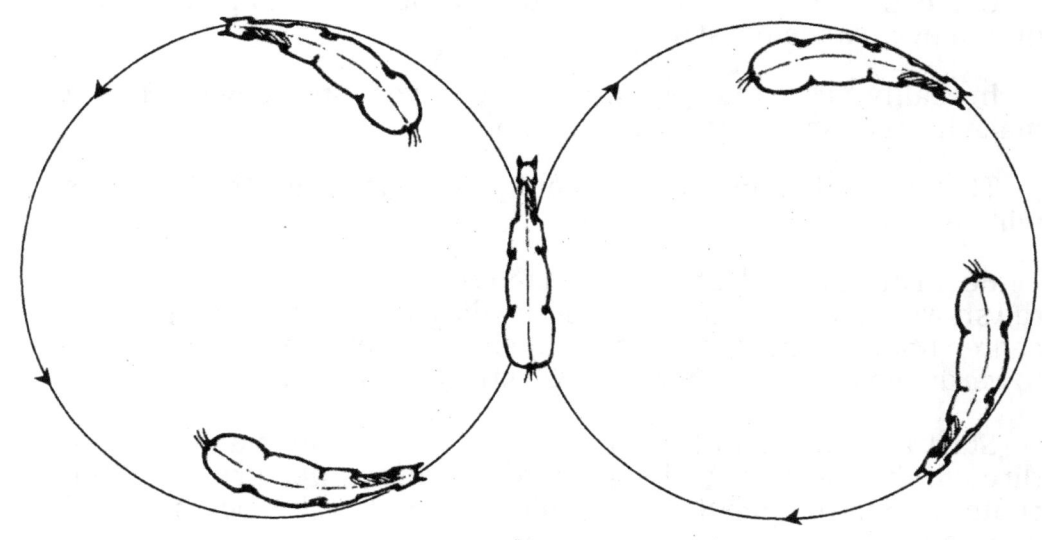

You can do 2 small circles hindquarters-in with some steps forward and very straight when changing from one circle to the next.

Half-pass

This movement can be one of the most elegant movements a horse can perform.

Correctly done, he can seem to float across the manege as if drawn by an invisible string.

In reality, all of your preparation by travers and renvers should make it easy especially if you remember:

The better the bend in the shoulder-in, the easier the half-pass will be.

Begin at walk and later at collected trot, ride a 10 meter circle at the short end of the *manège* as in the diagram. On returning to the center line, do one or two steps of shoulder-in and then half-pass towards the long side, then proceed straight ahead and reward.

Start a shoulder-in towards the end of the long side, continue through the corner and along half of the short side, turn down the center line in the position of shoulder-in, and in this position, and maintaining your aids for shoulder-in, add hindquarters-in to it, and...

WOW! You're doing half-pass! Relax the aids and walk forward and reward your horse.

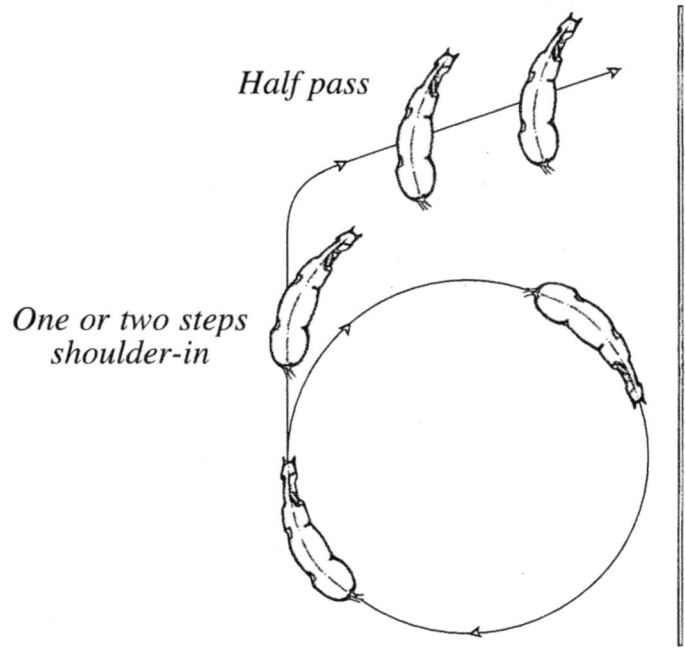

When you think about it, the hindquarters-in exercises on the previous pages are really half-pass on the circle with quarters-in.

HELP!

* I keep losing the bend and I know I am taking the inside rein.

This happens to a lot of people including upper level competition riders. The important thing is to recognize and fix it at this time in the horse's training.

This is a classic German exercise which can be a huge help. Look at the diagram. This basically helps to prevent losing the bend and subsequently taking and holding the inside rein. But of course you need to recognize that it's your inside leg which is the PRIMARY aid for half-pass and it will all become easier.

* He's trailing his hindquarters in the half-pass. Begin your half-pass in collected trot. Be sure your inside leg is obtaining the bend, and with your whip on the outside hip of your horse add the outside leg and tap with the whip. Be careful not to ask for too much sideways until your horse can keep his hindquarters under him. This is really an impulsion problem. In your effort of keeping the hindquarters under and coming sideways don't relax your inside leg!

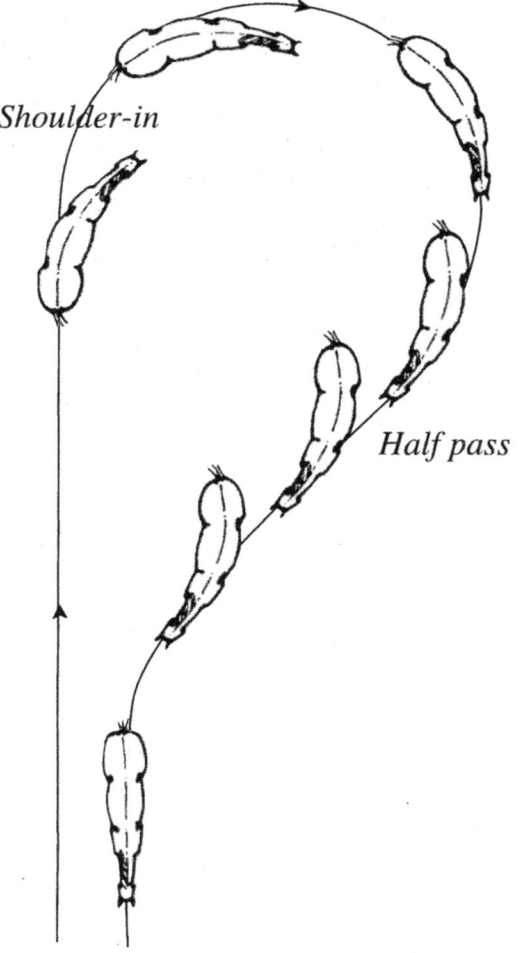

Shoulder-in

Half pass

63

* **His quarters are in advance [leading the haunches]!** This is the easier one to fix. Simply move both of your hands a little towards the direction of the half-pass and ask the horse to take bigger steps with his forehand. This will also encourage a bigger moving half-pass as he steps more with his front legs and also exercises his chest and shoulders.

When you can do these exercises in both directions and are confident you are not taking and holding the inside rein, you can develop your half-pass to include a counter change of hand.

To avoid the counter change of hand becoming sloppy and the horse leading or trailing with his hindquarters, in the beginning include in the change of direction a few steps of shoulder-in.

If you begin this change of direction at walk and think it through, prepare in your mind and practice it for a few days until you are very confident, the trot change of and in half-pass will be so much easier.

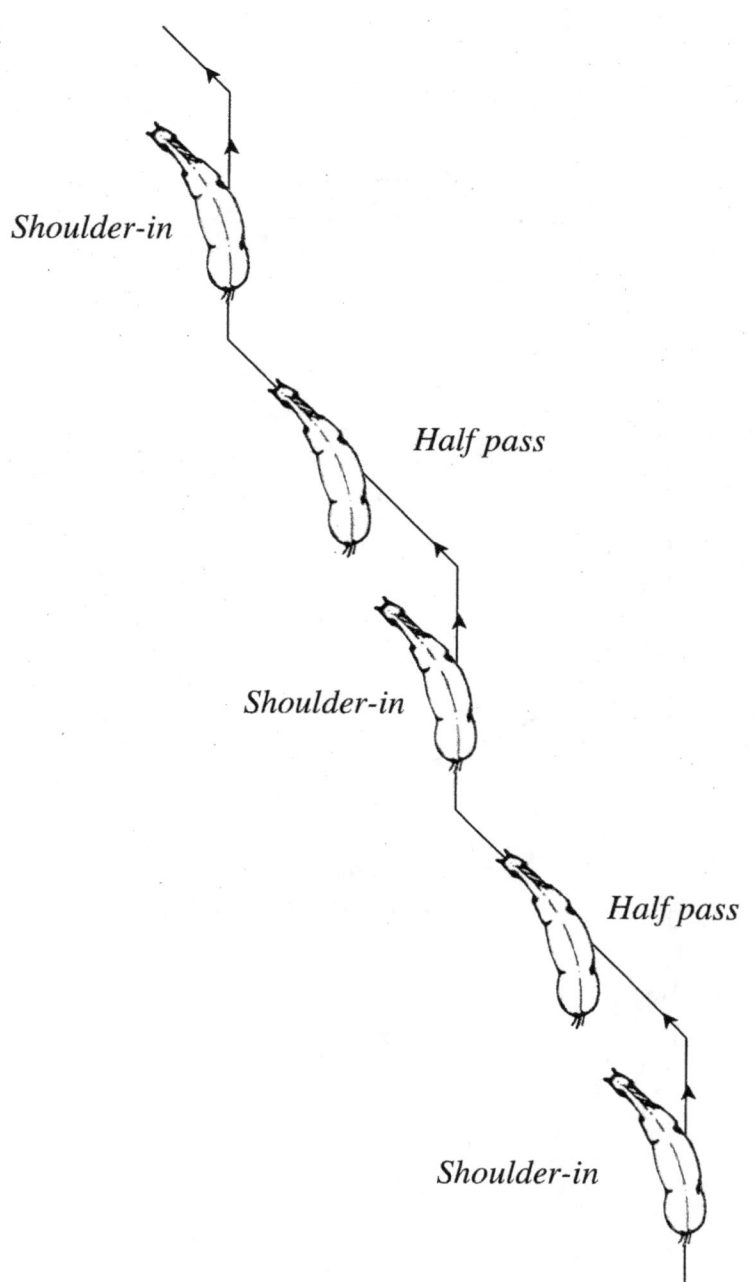

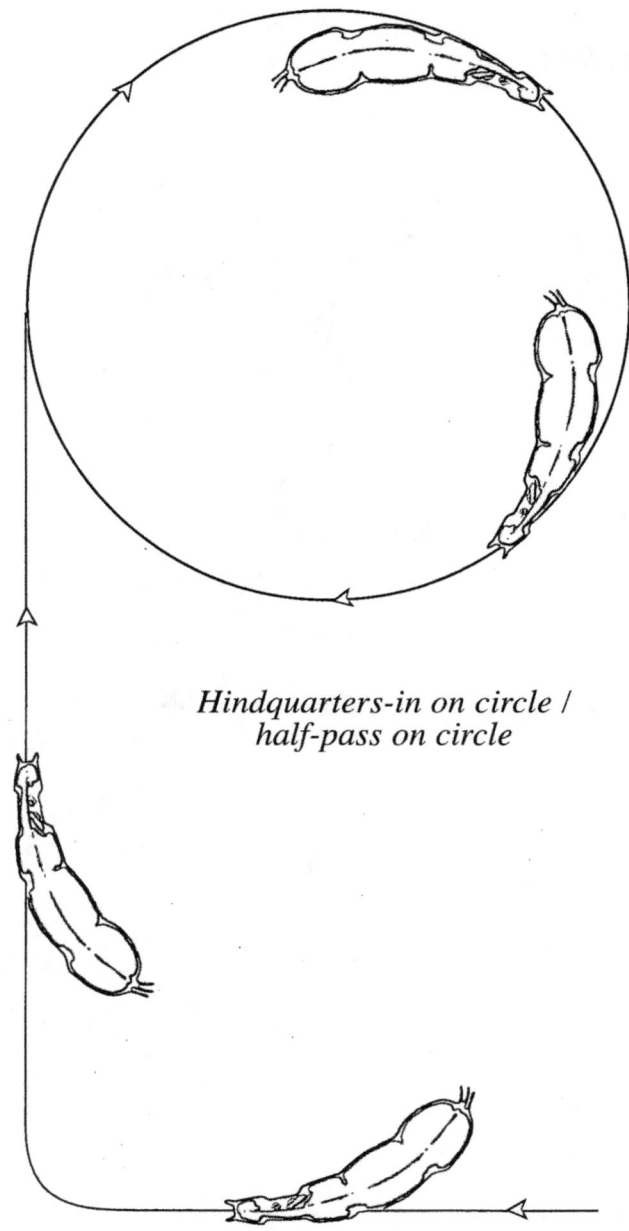

Hindquarters-in on circle / half-pass on circle

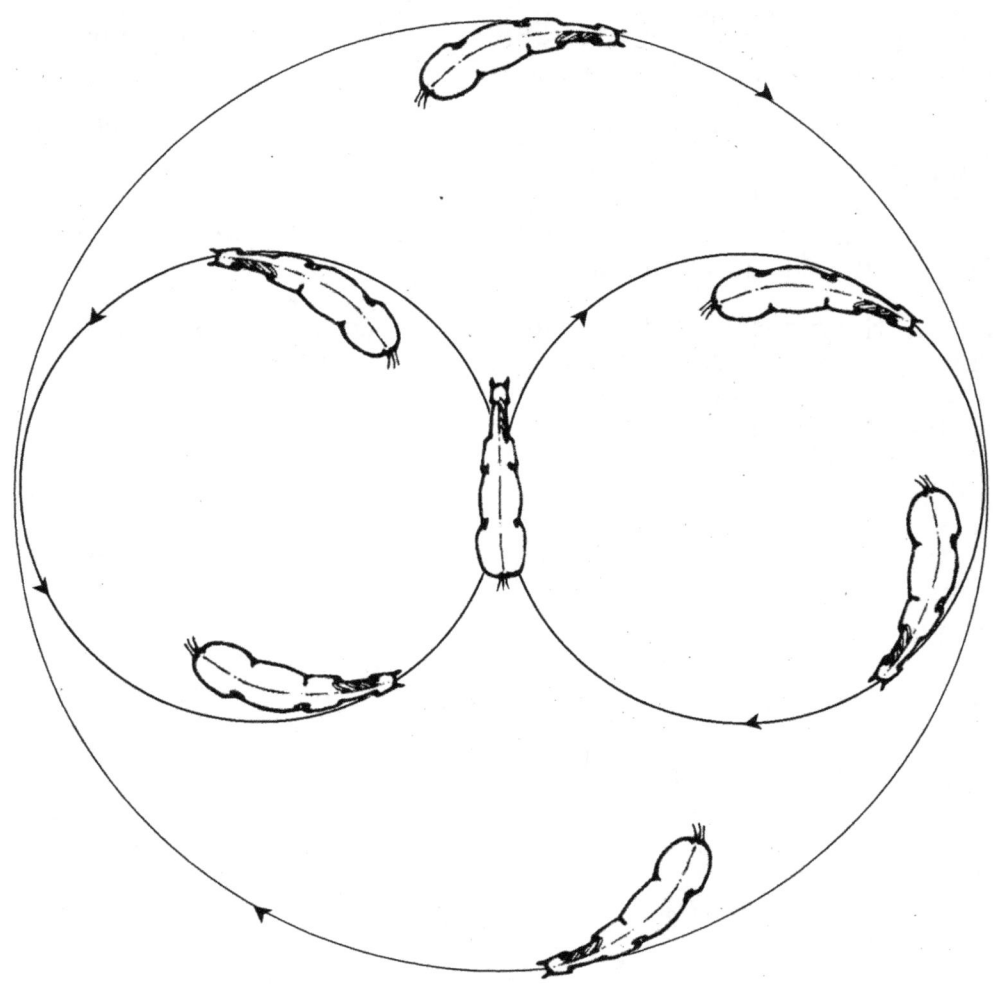

Variation of half-pass, quarters-in on a large circle then small circles with a change of direction

Renvers

This worries some inexperienced people but it is just half-pass with the quarters on the track.

Again you have to think it through and prepare carefully in your head. Looking at the diagram explains it. When you are confident with renvers, it is a marvelous exercise because the rider is thinking about the hindquarters being on the track and because of this, concentrates on the horse's hindquarters.

You can use this to develop a little "sit" in your horse. The following exercise does just that.

Trot 10 meter circles in travers [haunches-in], shoulder-in, and then renvers [haunches-out].

Look at the diagrams first, so you don't become confused! This improves your half-pass on the diagonal because here on the circle, the horse has to bend more around your inside leg and so the bend in half-pass becomes easy for him.

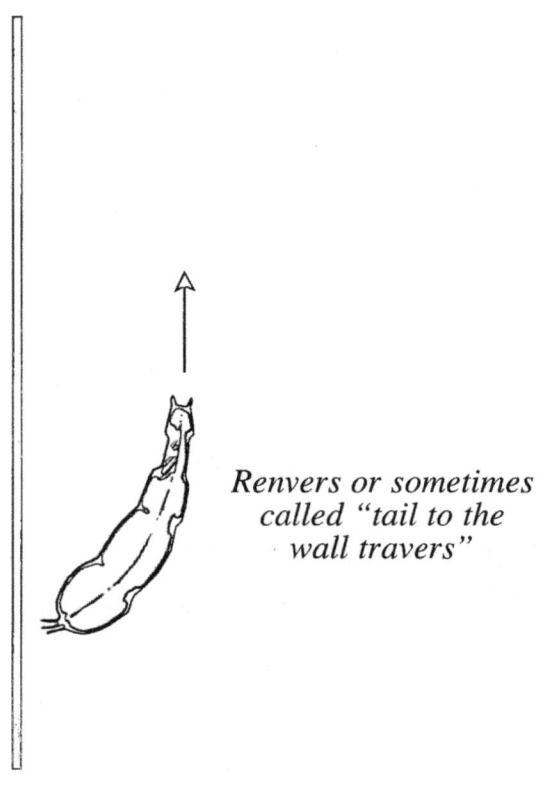

Renvers or sometimes called "tail to the wall travers"

HELP!

* He seemed to lose the rhythm! You need to be more forward and probably "give a little" more with your hands. Give / lighten the contact especially think about your inside leg

If necessary, use more inside leg; touch him on the girth in all of these movements.

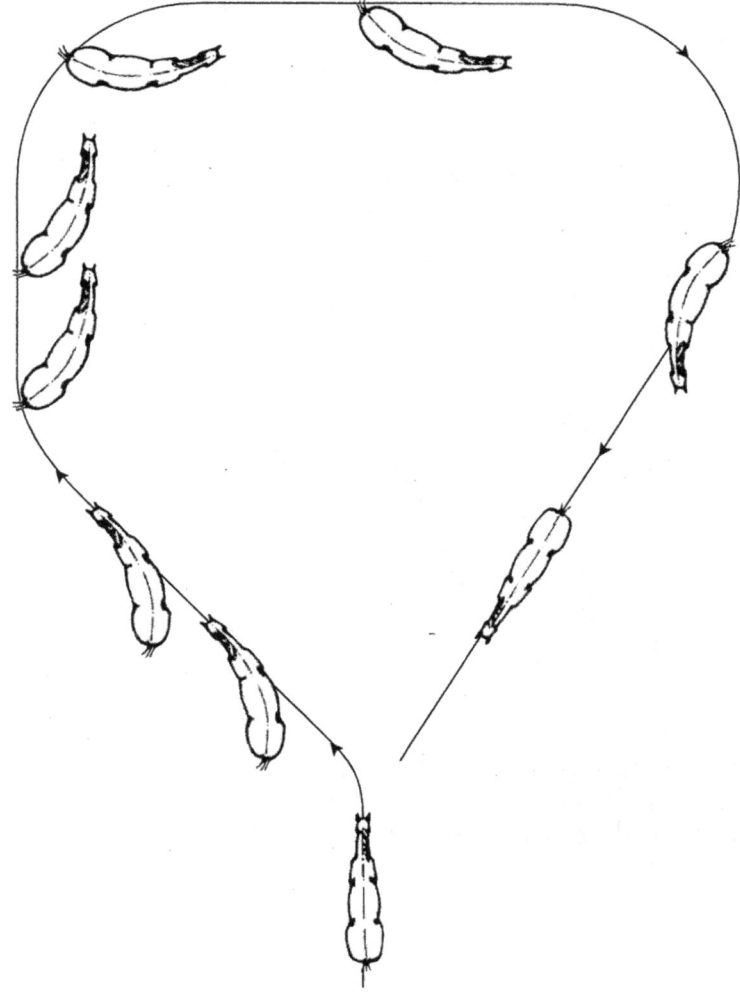

Begin renvers from half-pass on the diagonal

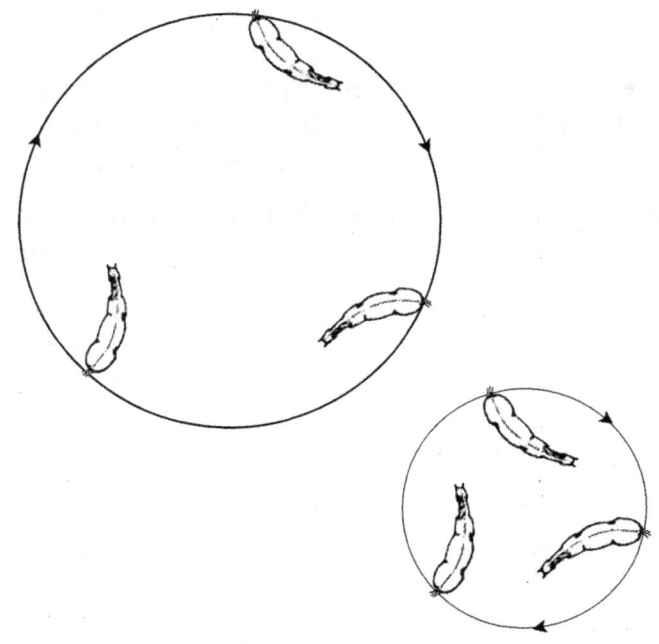

Renvers on a large and then a small circle

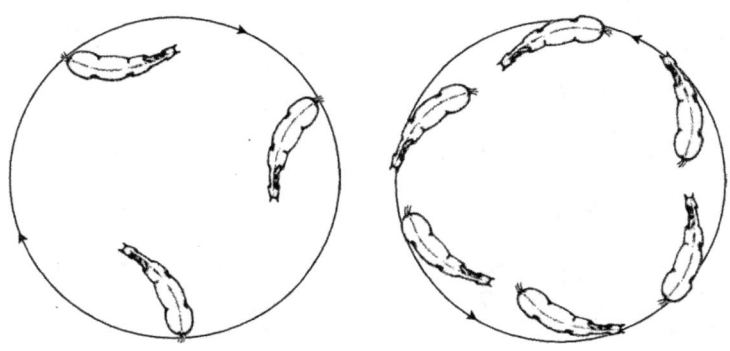

Mixing and matching shoulder-in, hindquarters-in, renvers, is very good for the horse gymnastically. The combination supples his back and his whole body laterally.

Small jumping and cavalletti exercises

Walk over cavalletti, beginning with only one on the ground and then add another [at the appropriate distance,] as if it were the fifth cavalletti.

The rider should have a neck strap around the horse's neck to save the horse's mouth if the rider's balance is not good enough should something unexpected happen. Then, if the horse's mouth was not touched he knows it was his mistake and not caused through the mouth being touched and he will rectify the mistake himself, if not the first time, then the second. The bridle should have a very soft bit. Do not touch the mouth except to guide him however wrong the horse may approach the poles or whatever may go wrong through the poles.

Having the second cavalletti (i.e. cavalletti number 5 see diagram on the next page) as a single one and not close to the first makes it easier for the horse to learn that they are separate steps and not to be jumped as one unit as some nervous horses begin to do. Then add cavalletti number 3 and later 2 and 4. As soon as your horse is happy and calm at the walk repeat at a slow trot remembering that you have to change the distances [between the cavalletti when you change to the trot]. You should lean your upper body slightly forward and take the weight off your horse's back.

If the horse is not calm or is rushing do not pull against him, just remember to do small circles taking your inside hand away from the horse's neck (i.e., open the rein) until the horse relaxes then casually trot through.

This is a good exercise for the horse's elbow and stifle area an on a long soft rein you can see his back muscles flexing left, right, left, along his spine behind the saddle.

The distance is, of course, slightly different for different striding horses. Perhaps 90-95 cm [35 1/2" - 37 1/2"] for the average horse and 1 meter [39"] for a longer striding horse at the walk.

Repeat this exercise at trot, starting at the trot with one cavalletti at the lowest height then two and so on. The space will be 1.3 - 1.5 meters (4'-3" -4'-10")[Editor's note: these distances have been corrected from earlier editions, per the recommendations in *Cavalletti* by Ingrid & Reiner Klimke, The Lyons Press, 2000 and *Kottas on Dressage* by Arthur Kottas-Heldenberg, Trafalgar Square, 2010] between each trot cavalletti depending on the horse's natural stride. Always remembering that the rider maintains his balance and does not touch the horse's mouth except to guide the horse's direction, whatever unexpected things may happen.

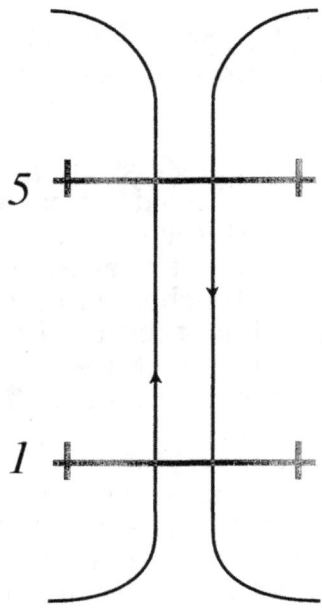

Walk spacing is 90 cm to 1 meter apart.

Long rein only touched for guidance

Trot spacing is 1.3 - 1.5 meters apart. Adjust to your horse's natural length of stride.

This is a good exercise to supple the shoulders and it exercises all of the legs as they have to stretch longer and [alternately] step higher.

These 4 trot cavalletti are closed up by 10 - 15 cm each from your horse's natural trot stride length and they are gradually raised to the maximum height.

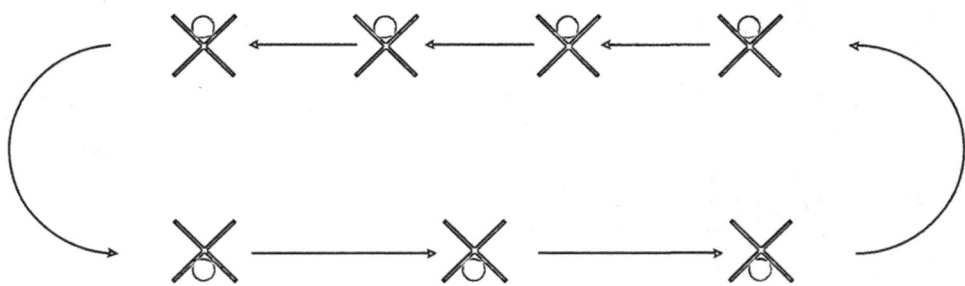

These 3 cavalletti stay at the lowest height and are lengthened 10 - 15 cm each from your horse's natural trot stride length.

Cavalletti can also be placed in a circular arc to be lunged or ridden over.

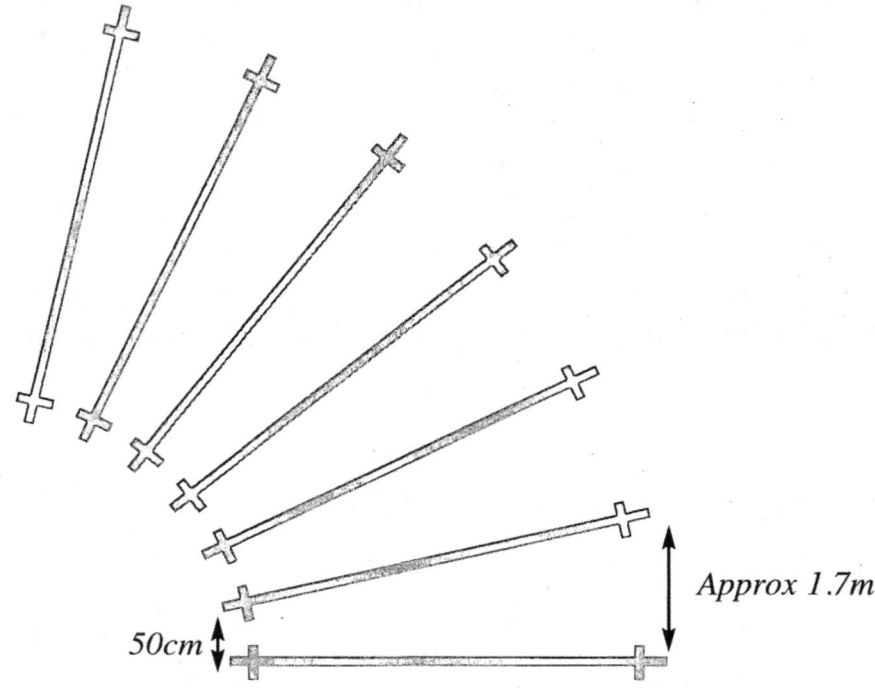

[The distance between the cavalletti at the center, where the horse will cross them should be 2'-8" at the walk and 4'-3" at the trot. Always adjust the distances between the cavalletti when changing from walk to trot, and back to walk. The distances for walk are not appropriate for trot, and the distances for trot are not appropriate for walk.]

Start of course, with one cavalletti at walk and when the horse will walk calmly over all seven cavalletti then start to trot over one cavalletti at the lowest height [6-8"], [then add one at a time, until the horse is used to them] and so on as before, building up to seven cavalletti at the lowest height [6-8 inches], before raising the height [middle height: 12-13 inches].

Small jump exercises

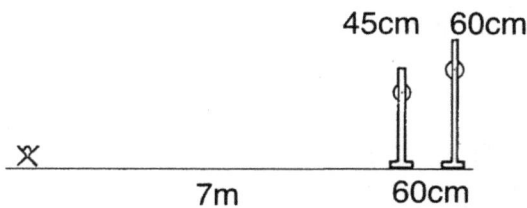

At trot, start with a cavalletti as a placing jump then one normal canter stride to a small jump.

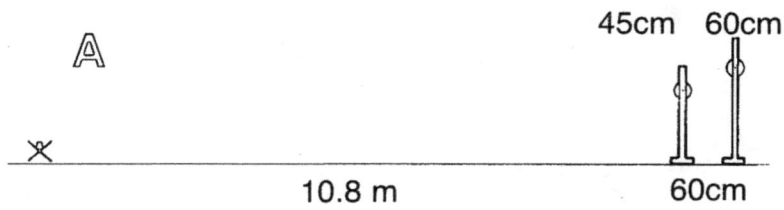

Variations A and B with 2 canter strides to a little bigger and wider jump.

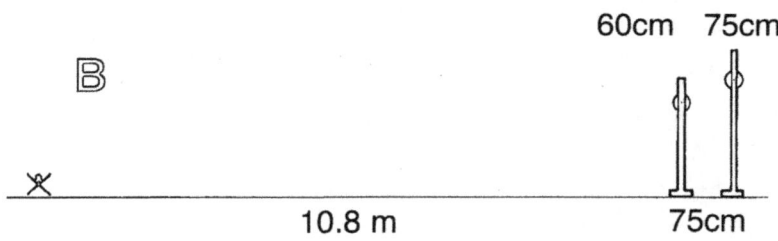

Put two cavalletti together and put a third one on top to form a pyramid. At trot, angle your approach and jump at the angle from both directions.

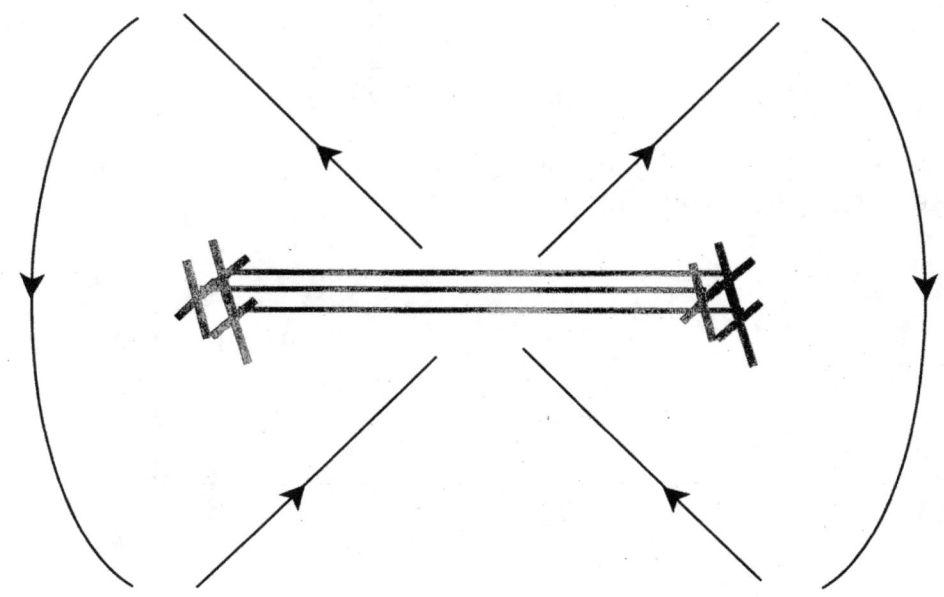

"On your line at your speed"   *F. Mairinger*

Variations of suppling exercises

Are there more ways to develop you horse's body?

Yes.

As well as the above exercises, there are some you can do outside the arena.

The simplest is very good for your horse's 'throughness,' his back, and consequently develops his topline and back and neck muscles.

Find a piece of ground about the size of your arena but with a small slope on it, not too steep.

Now with your horse very round, very relaxed in the poll and a light contact, SLOWLY trot, rising trot, some circles approximately 20 meter, first in one direction and then in the other.

The uphill strengthens the horse's back muscles, the downhill loosens his back, brings his hind legs under himself a little. Here the rider should sit a little more upright, to allow the horse to balance himself (if you lean forward you will encourage him onto his forehand).

On the two level sections of the circle [after the up-slope, before the down-slope begins and after the down-slope, before the up-slope begins] the horse has time to recover himself. As your horse learns to cope, you can advance to a slightly steeper slope. Your priorities are to keep the horse's rhythm absolutely even.

WOW! IT WORKED!

* He rhythmically, evenly trotted up the slope and he didn't speed up going down the little slope. He felt very relaxed, very regular and very swingy in his trot.

HELP! IT DIDN'T WORK.

* He slowed down going up and sped up coming down the slope. This is up to you to make sure the rhythm [tempo] is even and stays the same. Try a slower trot to begin with to make it easier for you, and use the two portions of the circle that are horizontal to help the horse maintain his balance and rhythm.

This is a more effective exercise than it sounds!

When you can do say 6 circles to the left and then 6 circles to the right, mix them up as in a figure of eight so you can keep changing direction, but keep the circle round and the rhythm even.

A variation of this exercise, especially if you live in totally flat country is to lunge your horse without side reins in a paddock with a dam bank. If you include the dam bank in the lunge circle the horse gets very good exercise up and down. Do not do too much to start with, it can be very strenuous and the muscles take time to build up.

Before you lunge a horse free like this, be sure the horse will not be 'inclined' to take off while out in the open.

Back suppling exercise ~ also improves the quality of the canter

Establish a trot shoulder-in on a 20 meter circle.

When the horse is light on the inside rein, sit down and canter forward, with the canter transition coming from behind. Canter about 1/2 the circle then the difficult part, gently come back to trot shoulder-in. BUT the first step of trot needs to be shoulder-in and as soon as the horse is light on the inside rein, again canter forward half a circle.

Repeat the exercise in both directions.

This is a very good exercise for suppling a horse's back and also for improving the quality of the canter because the shoulder-in places the inside hind leg under the horse for the strike-off.

This exercise can also be very strenuous for the horse. This applies particularly to ex-racehorses who can have previous back strain, so watch your horse's reaction and particularly don't do it too much, say 2 - 3 times each direction until you are sure it is not too difficult or strenuous for your horse's back.

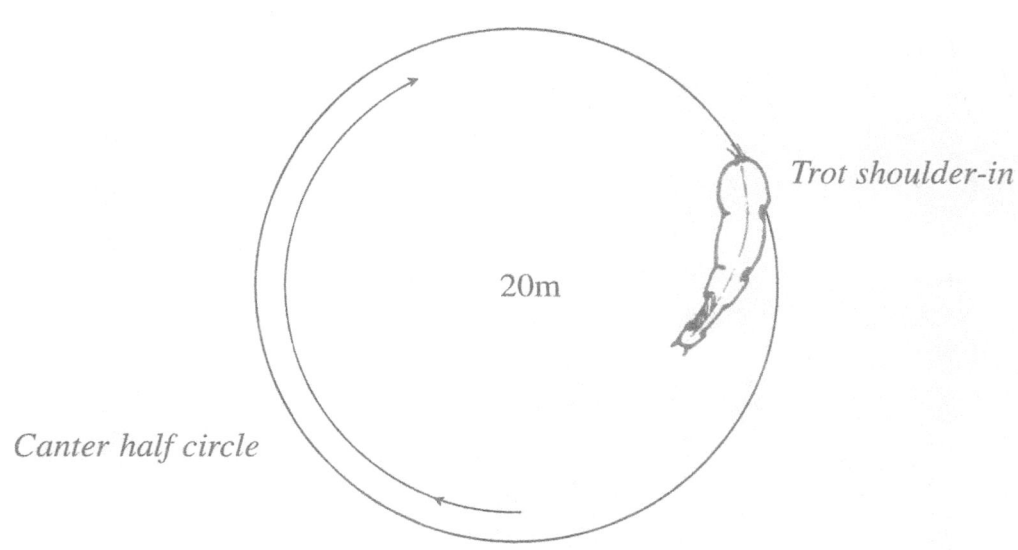

Exercise to loosen and supple the shoulder and chest muscles.

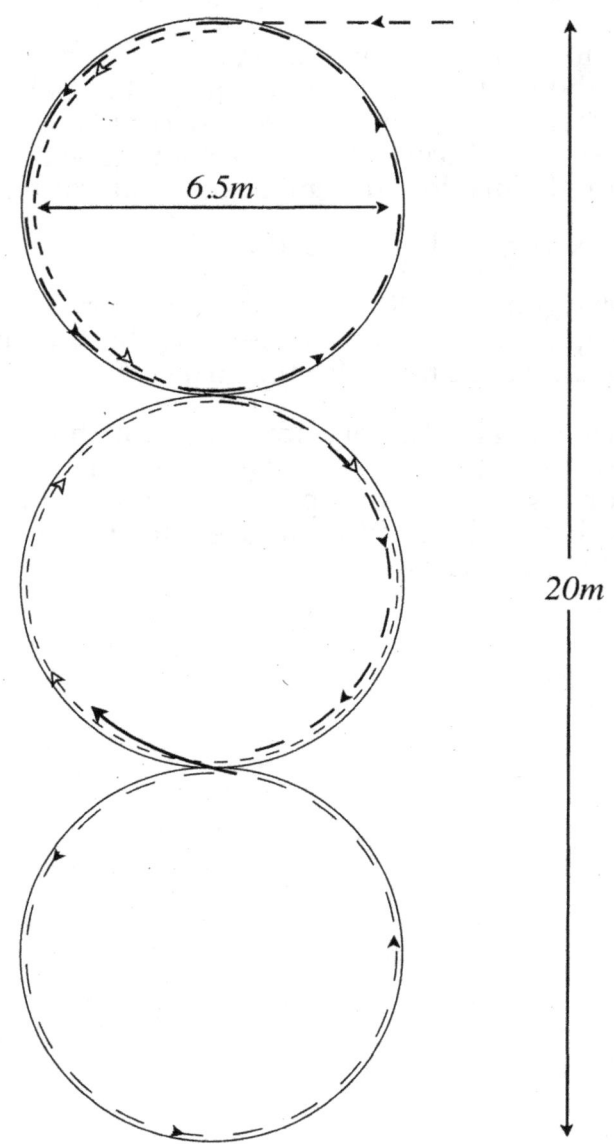

At trot across the short end of the arena, ride three 6.5 meter circles. Some circles have to be ridden 1 1/2 times to complete the pattern.

Mind Bender Exercise

This exercise can be a mind bender for riders. You have to be very clear in your head that you keep the same bend as you change the small circles.

In reality you walk the horse's forehand around the quarters and then the hindquarters around the forehand.

Your horse has to step wider sideways exercising and loosening his chest muscles, and then as the hind legs step sideways wider, you exercise the muscles between the hind legs and the pelvis.

To an onlooker, it is very obvious what a great gymnastic exercise this is.

Do this first at walk, then at a fairly slow trot to allow the horse's muscles to be accustomed to it.

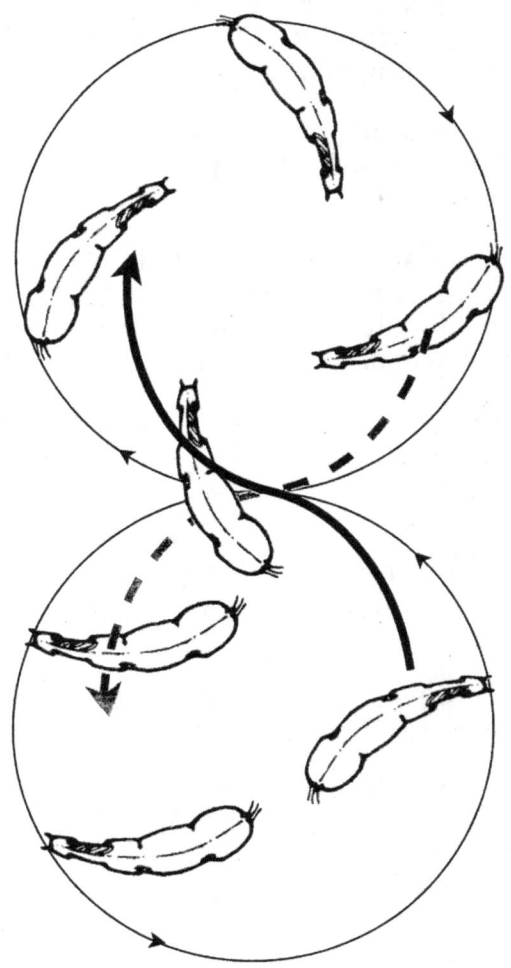

Transitions

"Not 100 transitions per ride, 1000." *Nuno Oliveira*

Always make dozens, hundreds of transitions whenever you work your horse. Working at the same pace around and around your area on the same track without any variations in pace, without transitions, teaches your horse nothing, and just makes him bored and he will probably begin to lean on the bit!!

Can downward transitions help your horse gymnastically?

Yes!

Because when you ask him to bring his hind legs a little more underneath him, this not only teaches him to 'sit' a little, but he has to bend his back longitudinally. That means he rounds his back, and these two things complement each other.

When he can sit a little in his downward transitions, this helps his collection because he has already learned to flex all the joints in his hind legs.

So how do you teach your horse to do his downward transitions from behind which is where they must originate just the same as your upwards transitions? It is difficult to understand this when your rein and hands are there and so easy to use.

And the only way to believe this is to try. It is difficult to begin with, so give your aids in the sequence of

1. Weight down

2. Gently flex your fingers and most important as soon as you feel your horse answer your aids *stop asking* so he knows he's doing what you want.

3. And lastly gently close your legs to keep the hind legs coming for the next gait/pace or halt.

This all sounds like too many details! But if you persevere, begin going from trot to walk and do it 1, 2, 3 and you are, again that word, CONSISTENT.

Very soon you will find that your horse is really pretty smart and he's beginning to come from trot to walk as soon as you make yourself heavy in the saddle. You almost don't need your hand aid at all.

Next you will FEEL him 'sit' a little as he, because the transition is coming from behind, brings his hind legs in underneath his body a little.

WOW!

* It happened just like that after you'd only tried to do it 6 or 7 times. You really felt him sit a little and didn't need to use your reins. SMART horse and GREAT FEELING rider because you were PATIENT and CONSISTENT.

Don't forget to reward your horse with a caress and give yourself a gold star!

HELP! It didn't happen!

* **You really didn't understand weight down.** Begin by making it a little easier for yourself. Start with rising trot and when you sit and make yourself a little heavy, it will be a bigger difference for your horse to feel on his back, and you think 'walk'.

* **You can't get the hang of sitting down!** Try to take a very deep breath and let it out as you sit down. Don't collapse or lean back in your position. Just relax downwards, feel your seat bones more into the saddle.

* **You've used all the aids and he didn't walk** when you wanted to go from trot to walk. Think about your hand aid and do it the in sequence of

1. Rising trot, deep breath, breathe out as you sit down.

2. Flex and close your fingers.

3. Repeat a little stronger as if you were squeezing as sponge.
4. Now insist that he walk, but be very quick to give as soon as he responds and walks.

When you can feel he is going from trot to walk by your weight down, you can progress to the trot to halt transitions exactly the same way.

To make it easier while he is learning, ask for these transitions with only 6 or 8 steps of slow trot between each trot to walk, or trot to halt transition. Make lots of transitions and in this way, you will repeat the aids many times to your horse and he learns them.

When your horse does his halts in his own balance from behind, an onlooker will see him start the transition, beginning a small 'sit,' possibly before you feel it beginning.

WALK

Your walks are

* Free walk on a loose rein – on the buckle of the rein

* Free walk on a long rein

* Extended walk

* Medium walk

* Collected walk

All of these different walks are obtained through transitions with the rider maintaining the same rhythm.

Horses should walk with activity and with purpose. It should not be hard to get a score of 8 for your walk!

So how do you achieve that walk?

You begin with a free walk on a loose rein.

When your free walk is active and has purpose, you will FEEL your horse's back move and to the onlooker his tail will swing relaxed and rhythmically.

If you can't FEEL your horse really actively forward in his walk he's not walking enough.

HELP! **He won't walk any better!**

* **He trots as soon as I ask for more walk.** He has to understand that you want a longer step in walk and should not go into trot. Ask for a longer step and as soon as he trots (this is not his fault) calmly bring him back to walk and on the first step of walk give a small kick to ask for

a more forward walk.

You may have to do this 6 or 8 times, but he will get the message and begin to walk with longer steps and you will feel this active, swingy, free walk.

* **As soon as you pick up the rein he offers trot.** You have to creep your fingers along the reins. You can't do this? Hold the rein between thumb and first finger and stretch the other fingers along the rein, close them, and then catch up the thumb and forefinger, and repeat till you have your rein shorter.

As you begin to have a contact, your responsibility is to maintain EXACTLY the same walk rhythm.

When you shorten the rein a little from the free walk, the horse relaxes in the poll and lower jaw and accepts the bit; he will shorten the steps himself.

With good lengthening and shortening transitions you will be able to achieve top marks as you go from medium walk to free walk and free walk to medium walk.

Transitions are what a dressage test is all about.

If your horse does a poor or even a bad transition and you accept it, he will learn that these poor transitions are acceptable. Go back and correct it now [right when it happens], insist that he does a better transition, and next time, yet better again. This way he will learn the transitions have to be as you say—GOOD every time!

Collected walk is not so difficult if the same principles are followed.

With a slightly more collected frame the horse will again shorten his walk himself.

If the walk rhythm is maintained and the walk step is a little shorter it has to become a slightly higher, elevated step and consequently a correct collected walk.

The rider's responsibility is to maintain the
Rhythm   Exactly   Precisely

Exercises for transitions and improving the quality of the canter

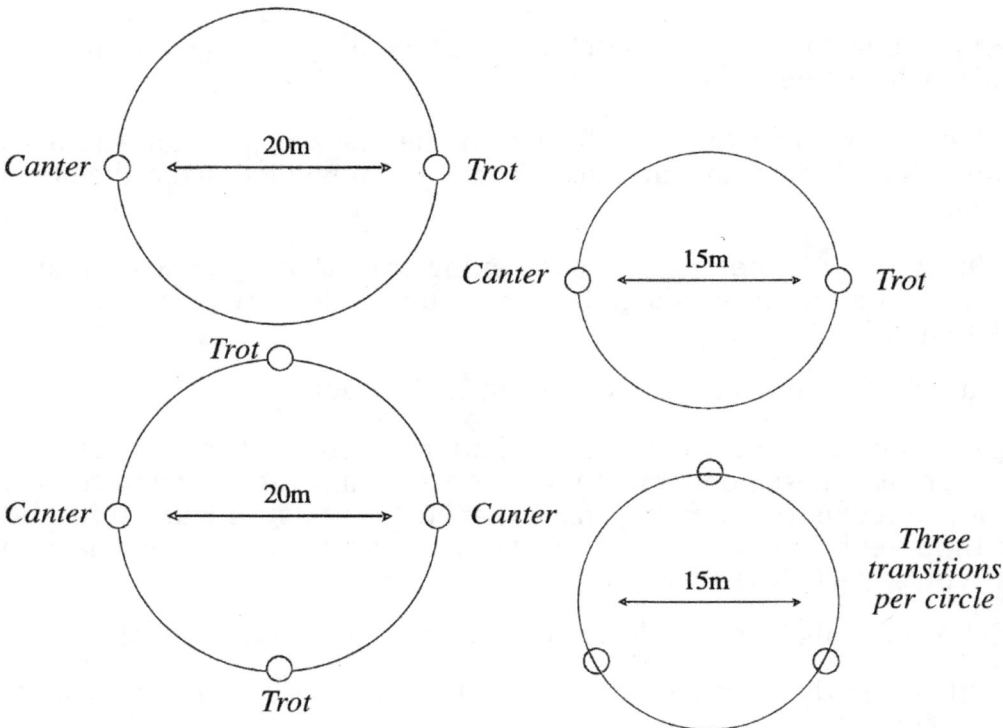

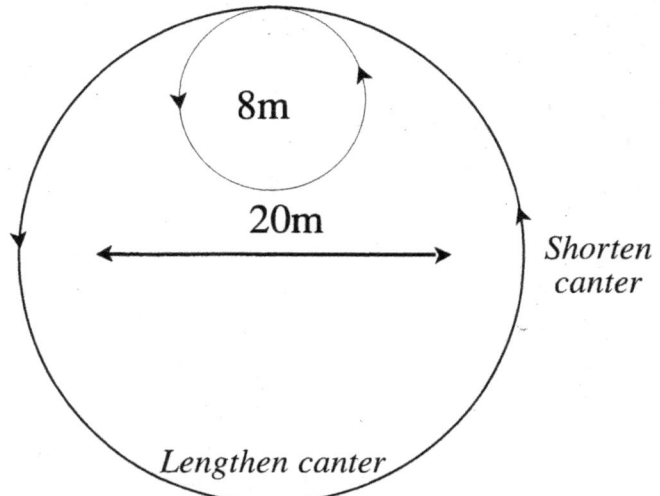

Working canter on a 20 meter circle and put one small, approximately 8 meter circle inside the big circle. Then on the 20 meter circle, lengthen the canter and shorten it again in order to be able to do the small circle again.

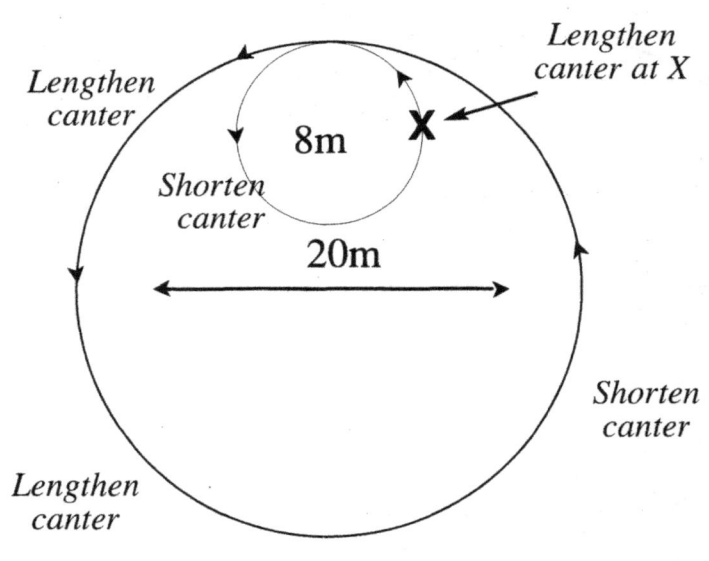

To vary the pattern above, in this diagram lengthen the canter on the last part of the small circle. This will strengthen the inside hind leg as he has to use it to push off to lengthen. This is very clear for an onlooker to see.

This type of exercise is very good for the rider as well, because you have to be clear in your mind that you are doing 3 different canters.

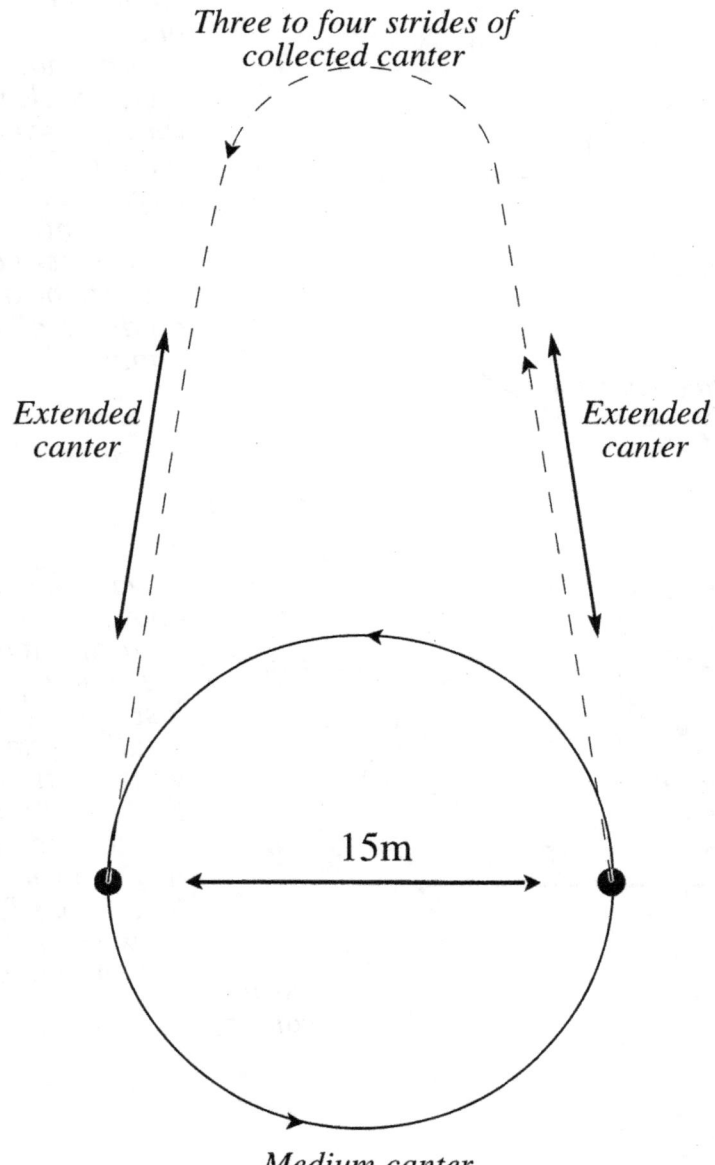

HALT

A halt is when your horse is immobile for as long as you want.

A correct halt is when he halts square, viewed from both the front and from the side. He is calmly and softly on the bit and at attention.

To achieve this, early in your horse's education you must sometimes stand for a while each time you ride him. The length of rein at different times is what you choose but should not be too short. And while you are standing still is a great time to develop your rapport with your horse. Relax and pat / stroke him all over with each hand and behind the saddle.

HELP! He won't stand still!

* **This can be difficult especially with an ex-racehorse.** You have to ask at a good moment, not if he is already tense or upset, and to begin with, not for very long. Talk to him and tell him he's wonderful. Rub him near his withers. Don't try to pat all over to begin with. Move forward in a calm walk before he wants to move. Gradually, as he gets his confidence, you will be able to lengthen the duration of stillness.

* **He stops but he moves a bit all the time.** You have probably kept checking and asking him to be square and moving one or two steps to square him up. Yes, he has to be square but if you keep him moving he will learn *just* that. The priority is that first he has to be *immobile.* If you come into your halts with the horse working from the hindquarters his hind legs will come under. He will sit a little and as he halts he will nearly always be square by himself. Your gentle squeeze of both legs as he is halting then brings a hind leg up [to square] if necessary. Again reward him, if only with a soft word.

When you teach your horse something new continue with your other work for the work session. Just before you finish, repeat your new exercise a few times. Then put him back in his stable with it in his mind and the next day include it in your warm up exercises.

Simple exercise using halt transition to develop "sit' in your horse

Your horse is now beginning to be a lot more supple. You can feel his rhythm in his trot. He is becoming more confident with your consistent aids and is working more in his own independent balance.

You can now make it a little more gymnastically difficult for him.

How?

Simply by doing your walk—halt—walk transitions on a slight downwards slope and later, short trot to halt.

How does this help?

It means he has to flex his hind leg joints a little more to bring his legs underneath him when downhill. He also has to flex all his legs when you trot and clear cavalletti and other small jumps.

Lengthened trot

Now you can confidently begin to lengthen and shorten your horse's stride.

And what will this do??

This will build up his muscles, his outline, his frame / shape. It is also the basis for your horse's medium and later, his extended trot, which will be supple, elastic and rhythmic. A trot that you will be able to sit because...

* He doesn't speed up and

* His back is round and he carries you.

Why can you be so confident when you begin this and how do you approach this exciting new phase?

You aim only to lengthen the stride within your horse's natural rhythm. What does that mean?

It means that the priority is that your horse maintains his rhythm.
* PRECISELY
* EXACTLY
* DEFINITELY

Begin in rising trot. This avoids you unbalancing the horse when he's learning, if you are not, as with most people, totally still in the saddle. Ask only for approximately 7-15 cm (3"-6") lengthening of stride, NOT MORE and only for say, four to six strides.

Don't ask if your horse is not 'through' and round in his own balance. He can't learn it if his back is flat or hollow so make sure he is relaxed in the poll & lower jaw, round in his body and don't over-push him.

Don't ask for too much or for too long...he's not strong enough and you will lose the rhythm, his head will come up, his back will flatten (drop) and he will begin to run!

But if he gets it right, WOW!

Pat him, tell him he's wonderful and ask for 3 -6 more strides of the same. Later, you use this basis to build on and lengthen the trot more, NEVER allowing the rhythm to change and become quicker or worse, even running.

If it still didn't work be patient; it will work. When you have developed the slightly bigger trot, keep that trot as your basic trot and lengthen from there and so on until he understands lengthening within his rhythm and not hurrying. Later you can apply this from collection and the horse will do a true extended trot from behind with his hind legs well under him.

In an arena you should be able to lengthen and shorten twice per [long] side or twice on the diagonal, not more, as it would be too much for the young horse's back.

If you have a young horse who offers a generous extended trot, take care; if you allow too much he will come on his forehand, and will, in some cases, spread his hind legs. Try to be patient and only ask for a little so that despite his ability to look good, he will remain engaged with his hind legs under him.

With canter, it's just the same. You still only ask for longer canter strides within his canter rhythm.

But here, there is a different feeling. You must think and feel as if you are riding / bounding up a hill.

HELP! It didn't work!

* **You lengthened the reins too much and he fell on his face!** You just lengthen his neck and the rein enough to enable him to be just in front of the vertical and then, come back gently / firmly to the shorter stride.

And with lengthened canter strides it is much easier to begin on a 20 meter circle. Beginning on a straight line down the long side is correct in trot, but in canter it adds to the difficulty doing the transition and keeping him straight. So make it a little easier on yourself with canter. Begin on the 20 meter circle.

Your aim is to do the trot and canter shortening transitions more by your back and seat than by your hands. The rhythm must be maintained during the transitions not as you see with many horses coming on their forehand and also [mistakenly inserting] a few hurried flat steps.

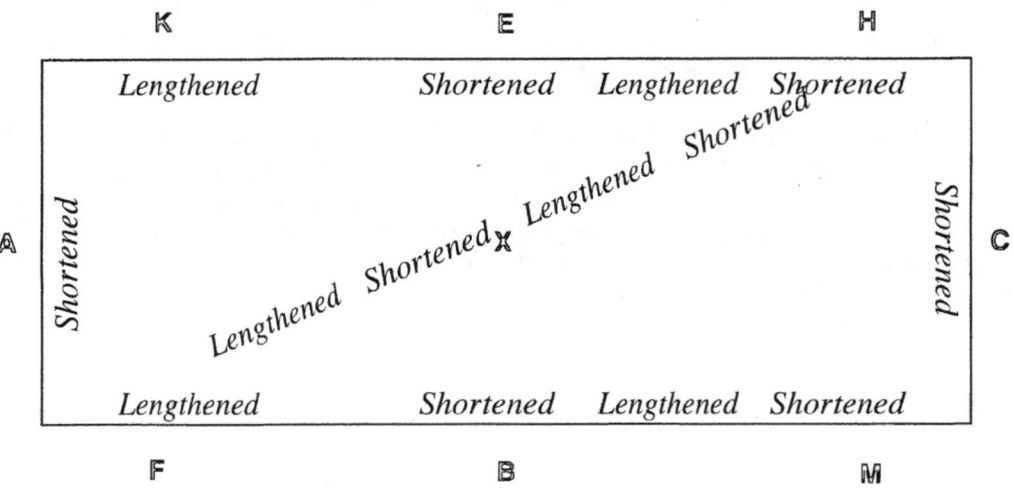

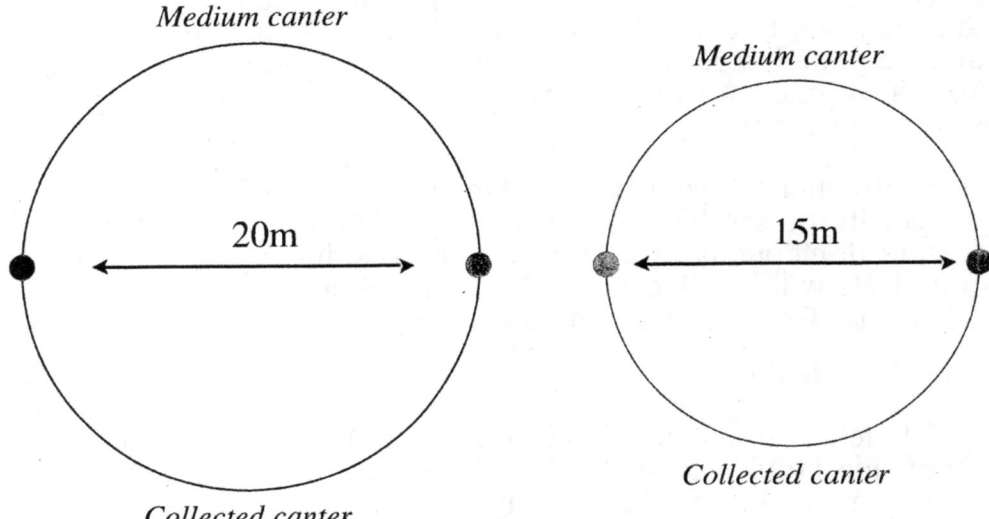

WALK—CANTER—WALK TRANSITIONS

The transition from walk to canter to walk is very important and is also a preparatory exercise to teach your horse flying changes.

You can help your horse by teaching it using shoulder-in at walk.

As in the diagram, walk shoulder in, for example, between letters R and P and when you feel your horse happy in the shoulder-in and light on the inside rein, canter forward on a half 20 meter circle. Upon arriving at the opposite long side, walk and immediately begin your shoulder-in at walk again.

Repeat the exercise.

After a few strike-offs repeat in the opposite direction.

I first saw this exercise at Saumur [France] and found it's a good and easy way to teach the transition. Your horse is already bending around your inside leg with his inside hind leg underneath him. Your aids [to canter from the walk] are the same as for your canter strike-off from trot.

Sit down using your back and feeling your seat bones as you sit deeper in the saddle and touch with your outside leg. Close your fingers, don't pull back, and since he knows these aids, his back will round. He will feel like a round beach ball underneath you and he will canter from behind, from his hindquarters.

WOW! He did it!

* It felt marvelous, round and calm. We just cantered to the other side, I took a deep breath and as I relaxed deeper in the saddle letting my breath out, I flexed my fingers and he walked and I was able to immediately begin the next shoulder-in at walk.

HELP! It didn't happen!

* **He trotted and wouldn't canter.** Go back to the beginning, same side of the arena and give your aids a little stronger. Remember to sit up and in and do not lean forward into canter.

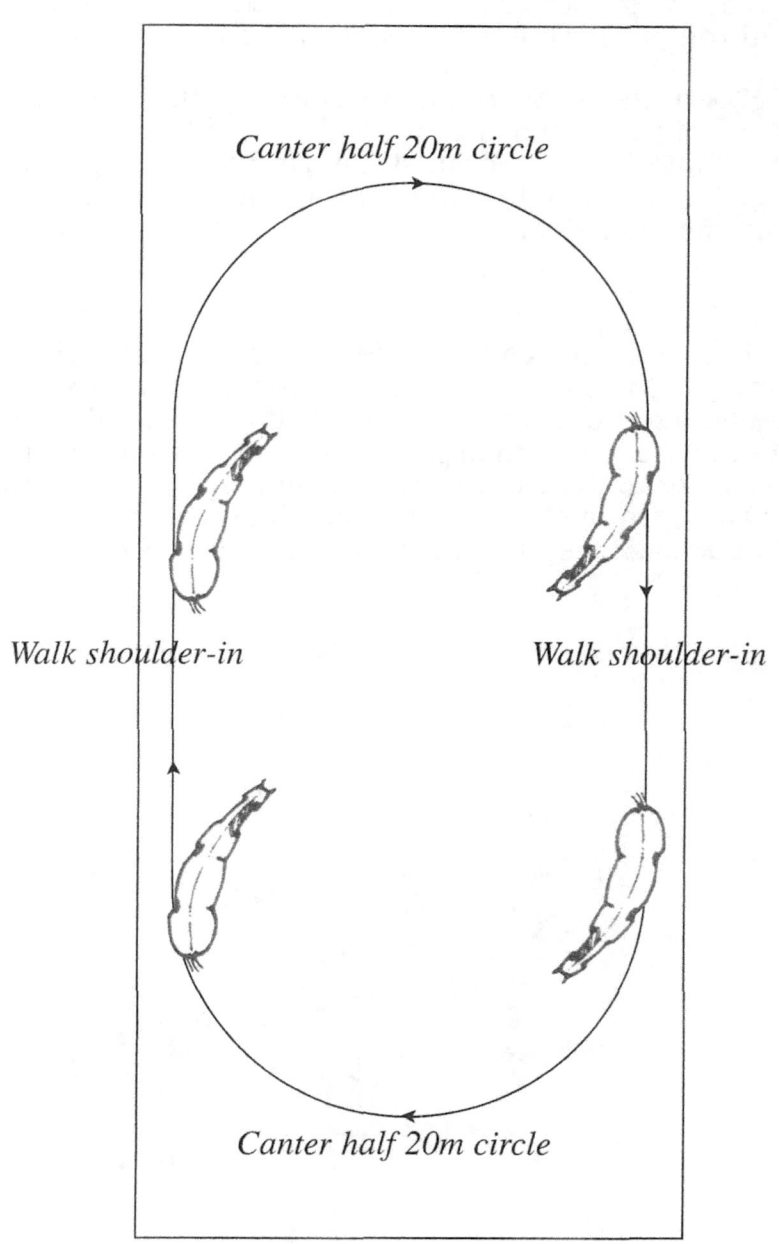

* **He struck off on the wrong leg [wrong lead].** You must have lost the bend that the shoulder-in had given you. Only ask for the canter when he is bending around your inside leg and your inside rein is light, look ahead at the half circle track you intend to take, i.e., think of the curve of your track. It is always important to look through your horse's ears to where you are going.

* **He popped upwards in his canter transition.** Probably your fault, you had too much contact. You need to prevent the running forward into faster trot but still must manage to give to allow the forward transition into canter. This is not easy; it takes quite a bit of feel on the rider's part.

* **He wouldn't come back to walk.** Think of your earlier downward transitions and think through your aids. Deep breath, make yourself deeper / heavier in the saddle, flex your fingers once, and again, and then gently but more strongly insist. As SOON as he begins to walk, GIVE and add your legs gently to make sure he walks forward in shoulder-in. Sometimes this is not easy to begin with, but patience and tact will help your horse learn this quite quickly.

Contra canter [Counter canter]

Because it is very easy to do this badly, start with curves much flatter than necessary, then as your horse becomes more confident you can do the required curve for a bigger loop or serpentine without a change of leg [lead].

When our horse is in contra canter his flexion is the same as in the true canter, not more. Sit straight; look ahead, and with your outside leg behind the girth for EACH canter stride to confirm the canter lead with a gentle tap.

Your horse, which knows the canter aids, will not change legs [leads]. Ride the line as a very slight reverse shoulder-in. That sounds like a lot of contra, false and reverse words. Think about it and look at the diagrams. The slight reverse shoulder-in will keep the horse's shoulders in front of the hindquarters and basically straight with only flexion in his contra canter.

WOW! IT WORKED!!

* He cantered on the false [counter] canter through a shallow loop down one side of the arena and then a deeper loop on the next long side.

Wonderful! Give him a pat!

HELP!

* **He fell onto his outside shoulder.** You took the inside rein and had too much flexion [mistakenly, in an effort] to try to keep the false canter. His opposite shoulder [outside from the bend] bulged out putting [more, or excess] weight on the forehand of this [non-leading] shoulder.

* **His quarters keep coming in.** This is [caused by] too much outside leg from you. Remember your horse knows hindquarters-in. Only give little touches [with your outside leg] just enough to confirm the canter [but not so much that you displace his haunches inward].

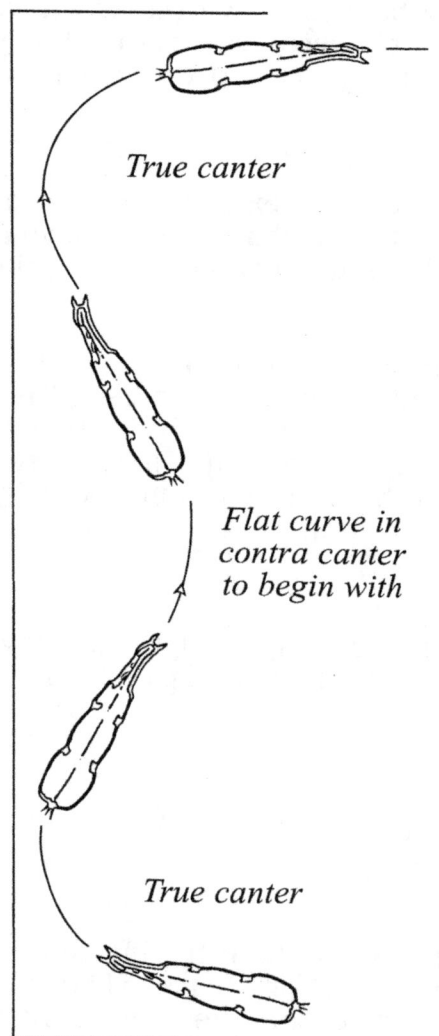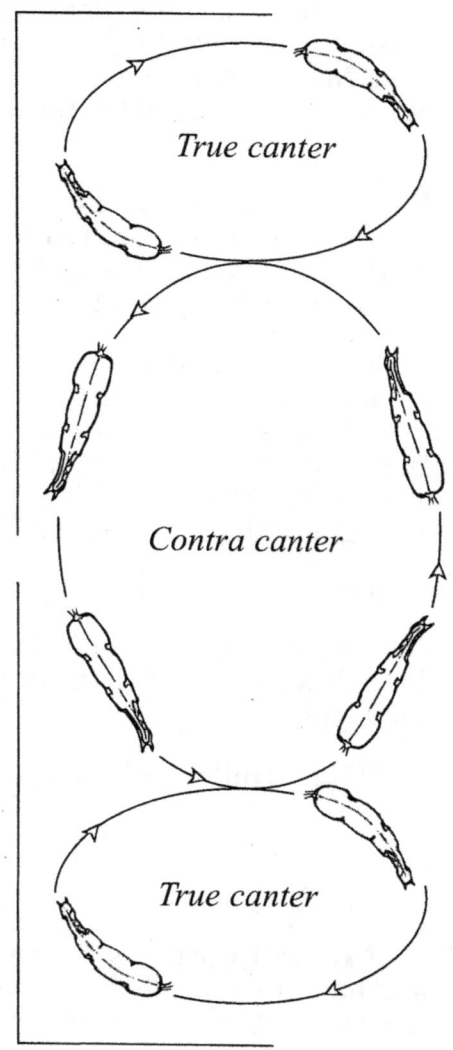

This exercise improves the quality and 'sit' in the canter.

Begin at A in the true canter, follow diagonal KXM and continue in contra canter past C, and on the next diagonal H to F a little more forward in the canter and feel the improved quality in the horse's canter, a little more jump, a little more sit.

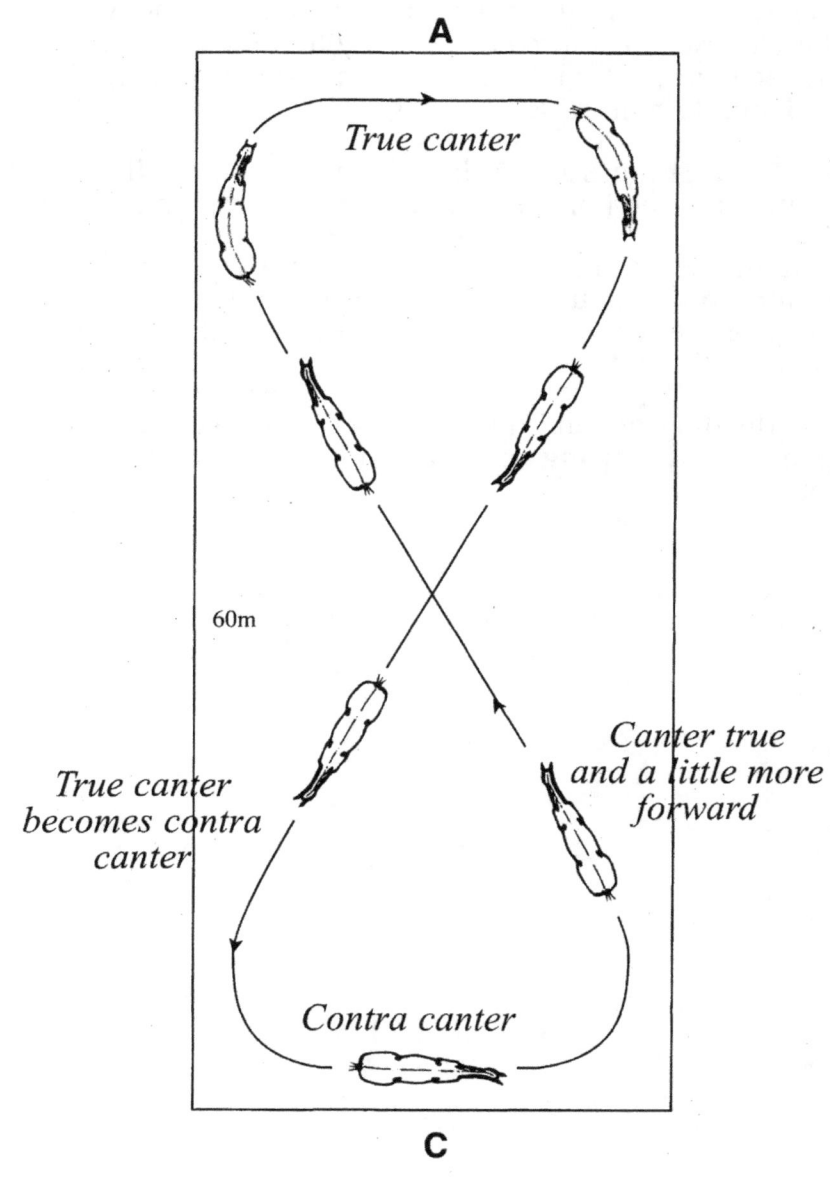

This exercise is proof your horse is straight!

Contra canter on the quarter line as shown in the next diagram and you will feel you are riding a tiny reverse shoulder-in say 1 – 3 degrees as you place the shoulders in front of his hindquarters. If you don't have a mirror, then have a friend help and tell you when your horse is straight. Surprised [by the feedback]? Most riders are. You thought he was straight!

When your friend says he is straight does the canter feel different? Yes! I felt that different canter along the quarter line when my friend said my horse was quite straight. My horse feels almost square, in the three beat rhythm. He is sitting a little in his canter of his own accord and with more self-carriage.

This straightness is the horse straight on YOUR line, which is different from the horse seeming to be straight on HIS line!

Sometimes riding 1 meter in off the normal track brings to your attention how difficult it is to be straight on your line without the security of the wall. Using quarter lines and the center line can be even more difficult.

Use the diagram and the help of a friend to be sure your horse is straight. It is surprising how many horses are almost [but not quite] straight !

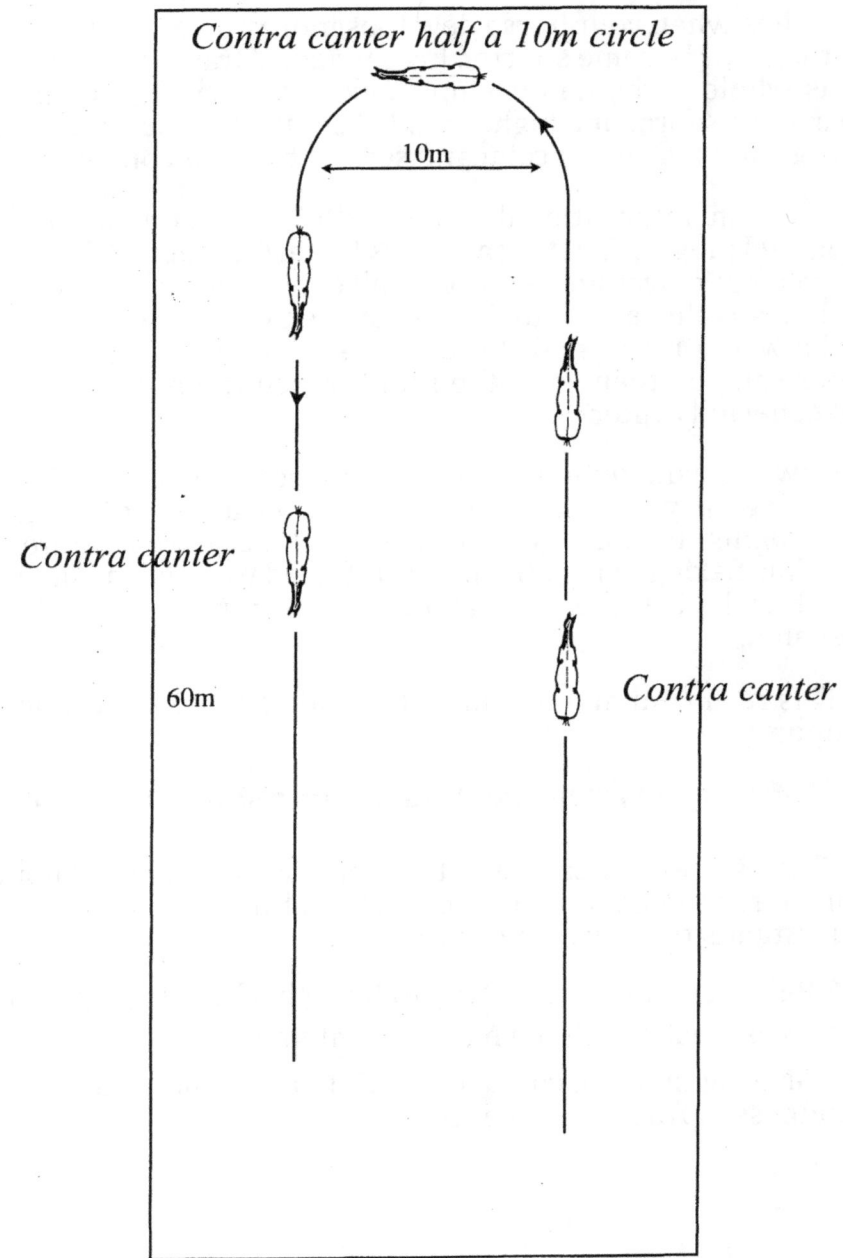

Collection

What is collection?

It is when your horse develops more power in his movement but the steps become shorter, his carriage / frame is a little shorter in his whole body; he develops some sit in the hindquarters and can carry his forehand higher, while keeping his back round, his poll relaxed, and his mouth calm and soft with a light contact.

At an international judges' clinic I attended, an 'O' level [Olympic] judge officiating asked us (smart) judges: "What requires the greatest power and energy: a full extended canter at Grand Prix level or a collected canter?" The answer was the collected canter, but he went on and said "When you have obtained THAT collected canter can you then 'give' the rein (lighten the rein) and maintain that collected canter?"

How do you obtain true and correct collection? From the beginning of you riding your horse, you are teaching him by encouraging the horse to work with his hindquarters more under him. This flexing of his hind legs is referred to as 'engagement' and from this, he can then 'sit,' allowing him to raise and lighten his forehand.

This results in him moving with pride and being wonderful to sit upon.

"Maximum from the horse, minimum from the rider"

There are lots of exercises to teach your horse this. Shoulder-in is of course the beginning of collection. Half-halts when the horse understands the aids, which are:

* Push - create more energy to bring his hind legs more under
* Take - resist with the hand to contain the energy
* Give - lighten the contact to maintain the energy and increased roundness of frame, i.e., the sit

The F.E.I. [Fédération Equestre Internationale] states that the half-halt is a "hardly visible simultaneous action of the back, legs and hand."

This all takes time and can be assisted by the transitions you do every ride you have. As Nuno Oliveira said, "not 100 transitions per ride, 1000!"

WOW! IT WORKED!

* You asked him to increase the power in his hindquarters but contained it with a momentary resistance (not a pull back) in your hand and then lightened the contact in the reins. He felt calm and powerful and in his own balance and [then] you could just sit there.

HELP! It didn't work!

* **He just slowed down.** That's too much hand, you did 'take the bit,' but didn't 'give.' If you 'take' you must give, i.e., lighten the reins.

* **He sped up and you let him lengthen his frame.** Try to ask a little less, push, take and give is just that, lots of little half-halts. When you give, it is not *abandoning the reins*. Light yes, but you must still have control of the 'length of stride,' the forwardness.

All of the lateral work exercises varying the length of stride, circles, voltes, in all work at walk, trot and canter, all of your gymnastic exercises, all develop your horse's collection.

If you keep in your mind the following quotes this will be a positive incentive and you will ride like a king.

"You should ride like a king and your horse must carry you like a king."

"Maximum from the horse, minimum from the rider"

"Ride with Power and with Pride."

Rein-back

There are lots of ways horses rein-back, but to do it correctly needs calm and patience when teaching it.

To rein-back, a horse must step backwards lifting his legs in diagonal pairs. Not step back as if he were walking in 4 time [4 distinct hoof beats] but [instead] in 2 time [diagonal pairs]. He can drag back, rush back, and step crookedly. But done properly, although called a rein-back, it is [actually] a forward [forward-thinking] movement.

That sounds a bit contradictory!

At a halt with the horse calm and attentive, squeeze and relax and squeeze again with both legs near the girth as if you were going to walk / trot forward, i.e., a clear go forward signal to your horse. Your hands don't pull backwards, they just lightly resist the horse going forward as if the door was closed in front of his face. If you stay calm and insist with your legs he will step backwards and you will immediately stop, relax the reins and reward him.

Done properly the 'rocking' [back, forth, back, etc.] of rein-back, walk forward, rein-back, walk forward becomes a single movement.

But you have to get the first steps correct when teaching rein-back.

You did it! Reward your horse and give yourself a pat on the back!!

HELP! It didn't happen!

* **He just stood there.** You need more energy from behind and don't get impatient and don't pull him back.

* **He dragged his feet back not lifting them off the ground.** Again, not enough energy from behind and you insisted with your hands.

* **He stepped back but went crooked.** Feel this [when it is] beginning to happen and adjust your leg aids. Move one leg back a little [on the side that his haunches are swinging towards] to straighten him.

* **He rushed back and wouldn't stop.** Your fault! Too much hands, you probably pulled backwards instead of just 'closing the door' in front of his face and allowing him to step backwards.

* **He's lifting his legs too high.** Someone has used a whip on his front legs [in the past]. Again be patient, create the energy from behind, close the door in front of him and you shouldn't need a whip for him to calmly step backwards. If you really have to, then ask a friend to gently touch him on his chest each step.

There is a simple aid you can use with all horses, particularly young horses.

When in a stable or perhaps being saddled ALL horses should have some manners. There is nothing worse than a horse walking all over you when you are saddling him, etc. Voice commands of...

* Stand

* Ba-a-ck

* Walk On

[These voice commands] should be obeyed.

The Ba...a...a...ck can be encouraged with a tap of your hand on the horse's chest. Later this voice aid can help you when teaching rein-back mounted and then the voice aid is discarded when he has learned the other [non-verbal] aids for rein-back.

Pirouettes

A pirouette is usually done at the walk or at the canter but it is also a very good gymnastic exercise at trot and piaffe.

A pirouette is a circle or half circle (half-pirouette) where the horse moves on two tracks around the hindquarters, which remain on the same spot forward or move a little forward.

The rhythm and sequence of footfalls of the gait / pace must be maintained.

To begin, only ask for a quarter pirouette and then walk forward. First, prepare mentally for what you are going to achieve.

With your horse walking straight on the track of the long side for example, after H, confirm the connection between the inside leg and the outside rein and sitting deeper in the saddle with your outside rein take and give a little to shorten the horse's steps remembering to maintain the rhythm.

Bring your hands a little to the inside, take and give and with your outside rein, move the horse's shoulders to the inside to walk them around the hindquarters. Keep your inside leg there [at the girth], and as you begin the quarter pirouette add the outside leg behind the girth to stop the horse's hindquarters as he starts to step out of the pirouette. Touch with alternate leg aids to keep the quarters active.

After 2 to 3 steps, walk straight ahead out of the pirouette.

WOW! IT WORKED!

It FELT like a quarter pirouette, he moved his shoulders to the inside of the track for 2 to 3 steps and walked forward straight ahead across the arena.

When you are confident with this 1/4 pirouette on both reins, ask for the half pirouette but begin with the hindquarters not staying exactly on the spot, use a 1 ½ meter half circle.

This will help your horse to step correctly with his hind feet.

HELP!

* **It seemed to be grounded like a pivot.** You asked for too small a circle a little too soon; try again with a big pirouette or sometimes called a *working pirouette* with the hind legs stepping on a 1 to 1 ½ meter circle.

* **His quarters swung out when I asked for more than the quarter pirouette.** Your outside leg wasn't there or was not effective enough. Don't press, [with the outside leg] just little touches / kicks. Put your whip there, behind your outside leg to reinforce the aid if you need to.

* **He slowed down in his walk rhythm**. Probably too much hands or not enough inside leg or too much inside rein. Your inside rein only asks for the flexion and then is light while the outside rein against the outside shoulder keeps the shoulder moving and controls the forwardness of the steps. It is your job to make sure the rhythm is maintained.

* **He doesn't move forward at the same walk.** Trot forward out of the quarter and the half pirouettes, this will keep him listening and thinking forwards.

One bad fault is, of course, for the inside hind foot to be grounded and twist as he tries to swivel around it [instead of stepping up and down with it in each step of the pirouette].

The Diamond Exercise

This exercise can be done at walk, collected trot and collected canter.

The quarter pirouette is just 2 steps and then, proceed forward but you use the pirouette preparation and aids, and then proceed forward and repeat.

It's good for the horse and harder for the rider if you lengthen one or two strides in between each pirouette.

The rhythm and sequence of the steps, whether walk, collected trot or collected canter, must stay correct and regular.

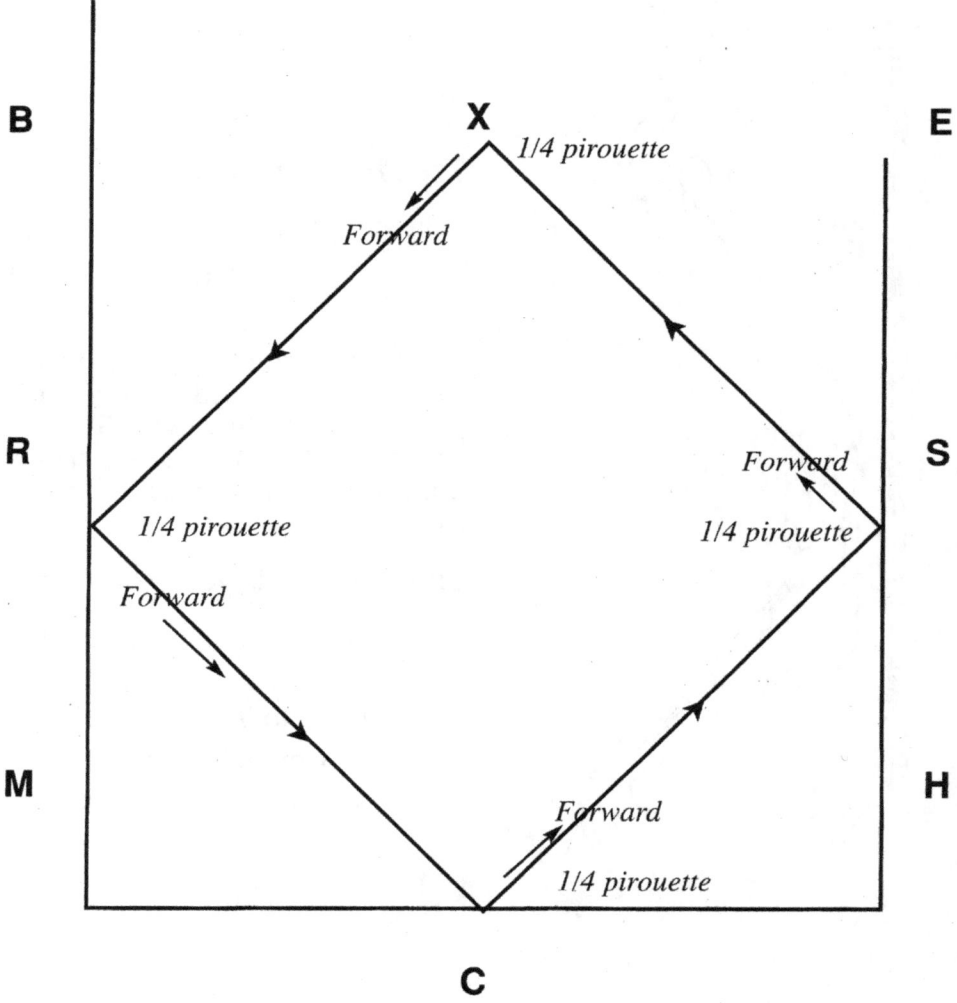

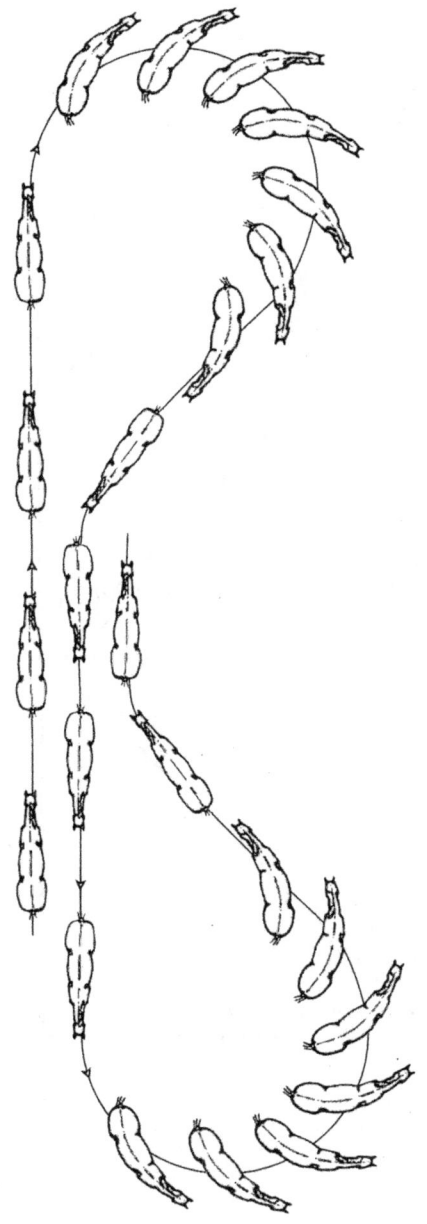

Trot Pirouette

This exercise helps the horse to bend his hind legs and to lower his hindquarters.

At collected trot, proceed down the long side and make a large half pirouette to the right 5 – 8 meters, return to the long side, trot forward and do a similarly large half pirouette to the left.

This exercise is very good for

*   suppling the horse's shoulders
*   encourages him to flex and bend his hind legs
*   improves his 'sit'
*   will also make him straighter

Canter Pirouette

Good preparation for canter pirouette will help make the actual pirouette less difficult. If this preparation is done during the horse's early training, sometime before you begin to school canter pirouette, you will have more confidence.

During your horse's training, here are four main exercises you can use for preparing for canter pirouette.

On a 20 meter circle begin with lengthened canter for about half the circle, and then the other half the circle at collected canter.

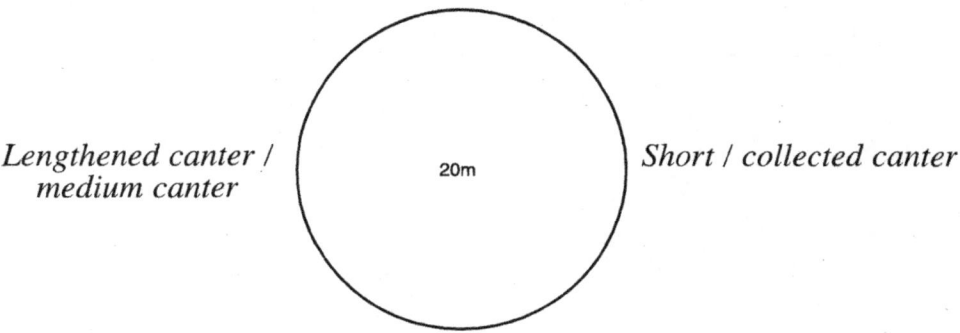

Shorten the collected canter to do one stride [of canter] on the spot then collected canter forward followed by lengthened canter as in the diagram. As this becomes easier, i.e., with a light contact, you can do 2 steps and then 3 steps on the spot.

Maintaining the canter rhythm and doing your transitions with progressively lighter aids will prepare you for a canter pirouette that will require only [the aids of your] back, seat, legs and a very light contact.

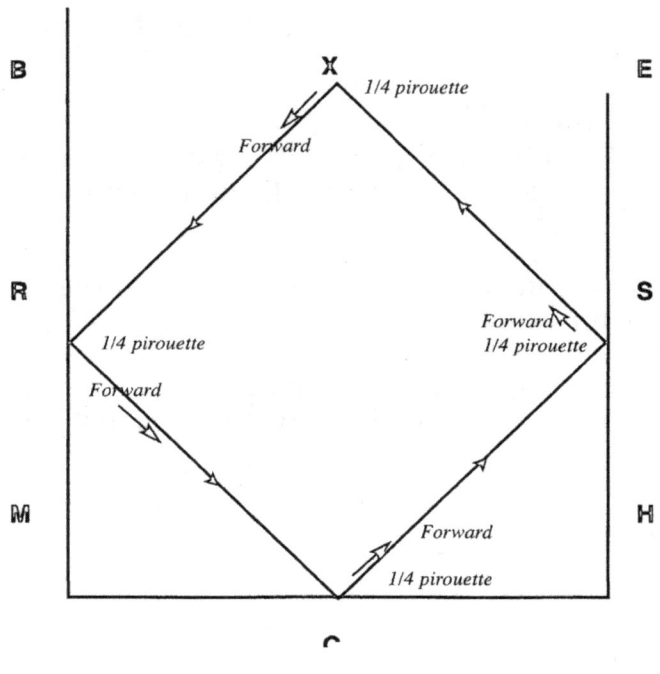

Doing this useful exercise at collected canter is a good preparation for the canter pirouette.

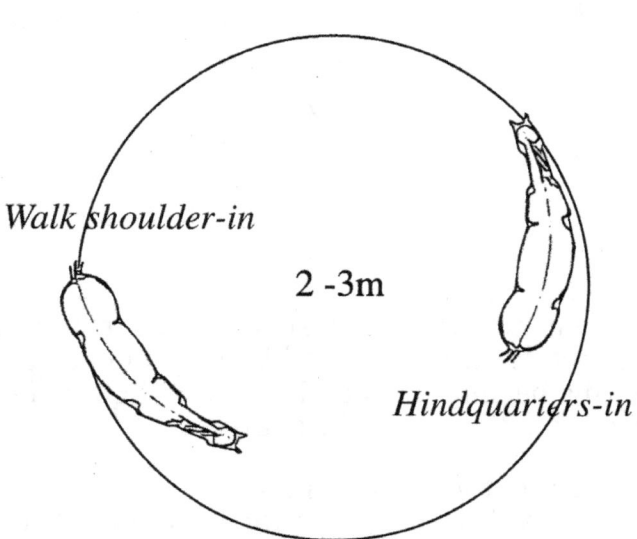

Once you can do shoulder-in and hindquarters-in at the walk, then do walk shoulder-in for half of the circle and canter 2 or 3 steps with the quarters-in, [this done] on the little circle and then walk again. You have just done a quarter canter pirouette.

Reward your horse and repeat once, twice more, and then repeat in the other direction. Very quickly your horse will get his confidence with the next 2 - 3 steps of quarters-in [at the canter] on the small circle.

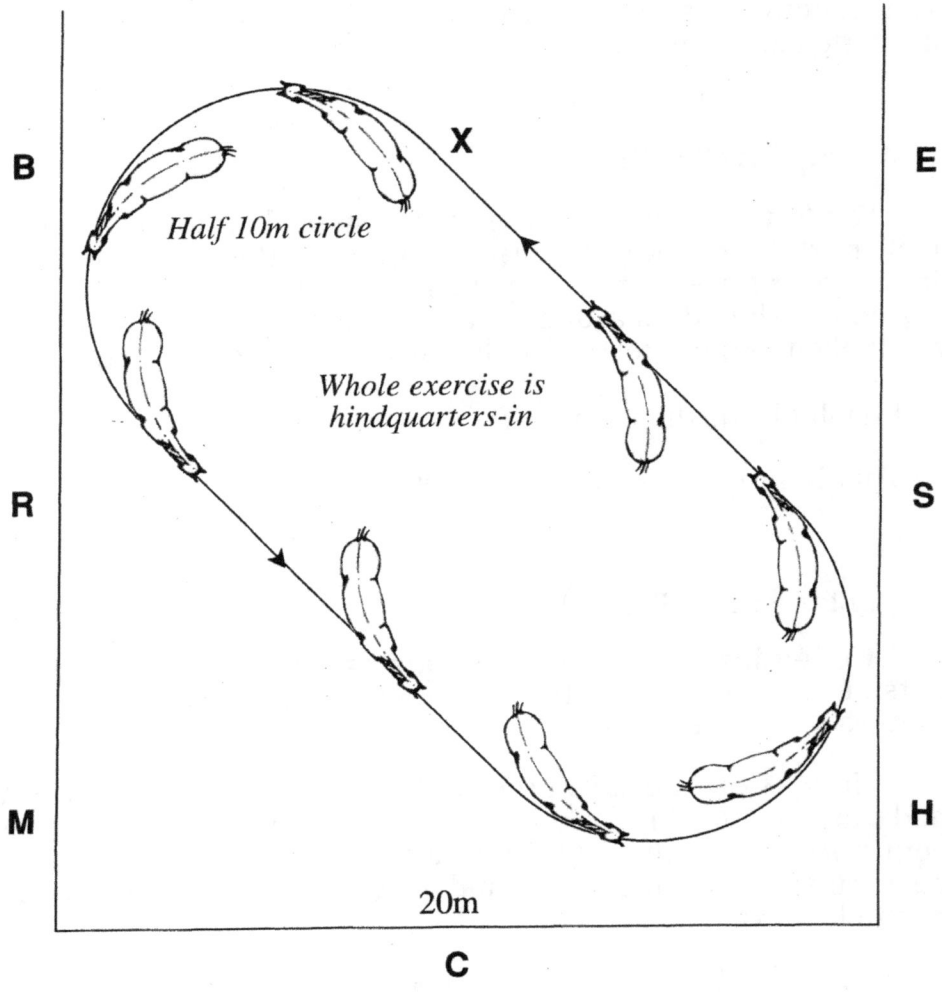

Canter hindquarters-in as in the diagram.

This is a good exercise gymnastically. The rider must remember when doing canter pirouette to begin with the horse straight / slightly shoulder-fore and not begin with quarters-in.

These beginnings of canter pirouette are the same as in the walk pirouette, shorten the steps, think shoulder-in and move the shoulders around the hindquarters, then after 2 - 3 steps, canter forward. One important point is that the collected canter into the pirouette must be the same as the collected canter out of the pirouette and all of it in the same canter rhythm.

WOW! IT HAPPENED!

* You 'sat in,' shortened the canter steps, had the contact very light, inside leg on the girth, outside leg behind the girth and carefully flexing your fingers, moving your hands a little to the inside, you moved the shoulders around the hindquarters for 3-4 steps while you looked in the direction of the pirouette but didn't lean.

He felt like he did it himself!

That is a canter pirouette of a horse in his own balance.

HELP! IT DIDN'T HAPPEN!

* **He led into the pirouette quarters first**. You had too much outside leg to begin with. The hindquarters-in exercise is just that—a training exercise.

* **He was on the forehand and lost the canter rhythm.** You had too much contact. You need to aim for less and less contact as your horse learns the canter pirouette and if your preparation has been careful, this will happen, and he will do the pirouette with 'sit' and in his own balance.

* **His head bobbed up and down.** There is not enough power coming from the hindquarters and the effort to lift his forehand is causing his head to bob up and down. Go back to exercises to strengthen his hindquarters, i.e., canter exercises with many transitions.

* **He didn't do a pirouette, it was a U-turn.** Go back to the exercises and also the trot pirouette to give you a feel for it and to encourage his 'sit,' [and to improve] the flexing of the joints of his hind legs.

Extended trot

When your horse has collection in the trot that is correct, and he has brought his hind legs more under him, he can flex his hind joints to 'sit' a little and raise and carry his forehand, and then your lengthened green / young horse trot can be developed into extended trot. This extended trot must be a regular, calm, rhythmic, elastic, lengthened trot, no rushing or hurrying. This extended trot comes from behind and the hind leg action matches the front legs.

The common faults you see in extended trot are

* Hind legs left behind. The horse's back is flat or hollow and the rider has trouble sitting.

* Flashy front leg action—this comes from forcing the horse too much, not paying attention to the action of the hind legs.

* The horse is spreading his hind legs. This also comes from asking too much of a young horse, and although the hind legs are coming under, the horse places them outside the front leg to save him from hitting the front foot and hurting himself.

It can also be a balance problem and comes from the horse being on the forehand when you ask for extended trot.

Exercises to develop extended trot

Shoulder-in on the long side for example from M to B or P and when the horse is soft on the inside rein the horse's hind legs will be under him and he can push off along a short diagonal up into extended trot. Finish the extension before his frame gets longer and before he falls onto his forehand.

Half a short diagonal well done can easily be built into a long diagonal later when the horse's back is strong enough.

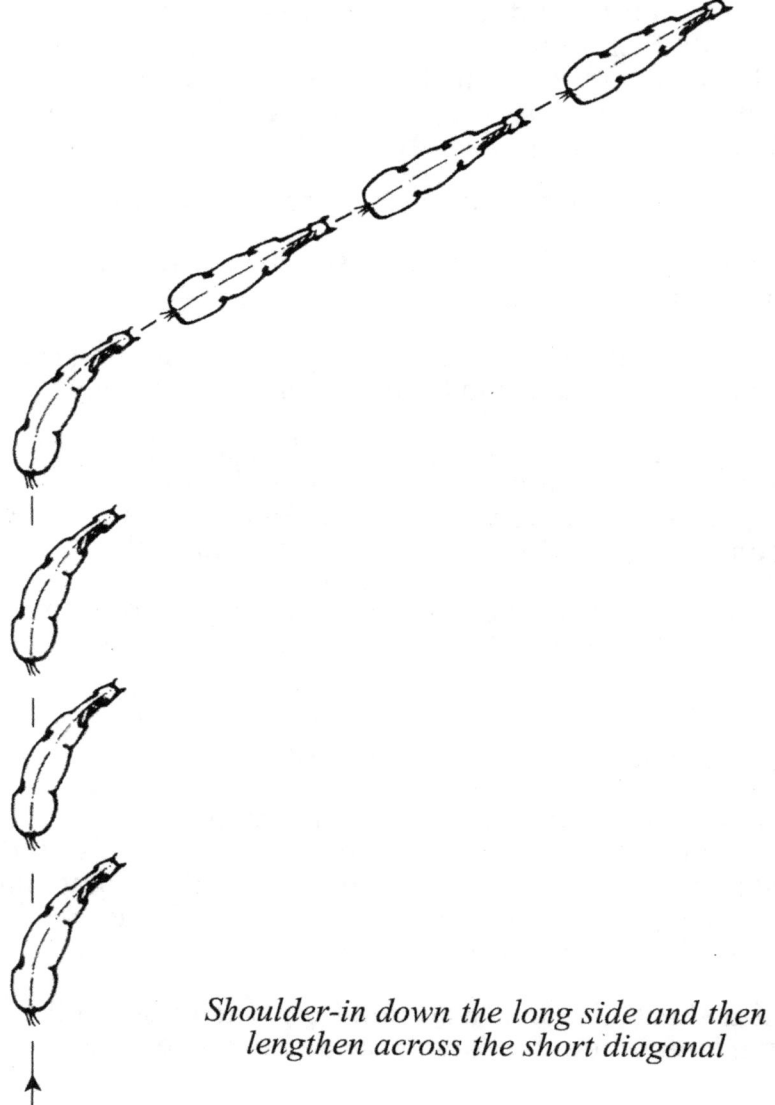

Shoulder-in down the long side and then lengthen across the short diagonal

When the horse can do this exercise of extended trot from collected trot with the easiest of aids and the smallest amount of effort on the rider's part, you can try another exercise to help encourage him to extend his trot with his whole body more off the ground.

Do a few steps of rein back. The horse's back is round from the 3 to 4 steps back and he can push off with his hind legs into a higher extended trot.

If you ride extended trot thinking 'uphill' you can feel the power from his hind legs almost right under the saddle as he extends and lifts up and off the ground.

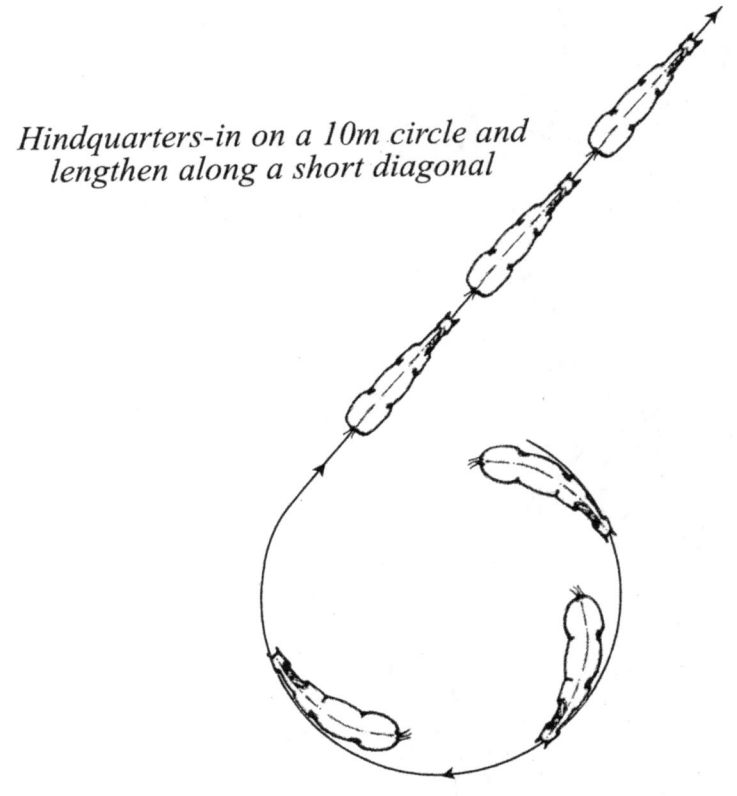

Hindquarters-in on a 10m circle and lengthen along a short diagonal

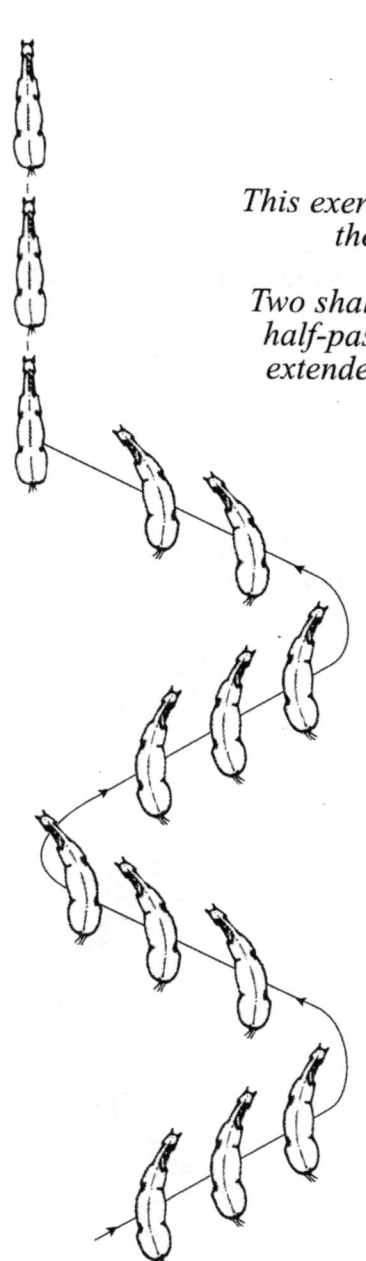

This exercise can also improve the extended trot.

Two shallow short zig-zags in half-pass before B or E and extended trot the rest of the long side.

Doing extended trot from piaffe and passage is much more difficult physically for the horse and all movements should be well established and calm before mixing them. The horse should be strong gymnastically or you will make him tense in the piaffe.

Flying changes

A flying change is simply a canter departure from the [other lead of] canter.

Not long after our much loved national trainer, Franz Mairinger died, we had a most perceptive trainer, Karl Mikolka come to this country and I was lucky enough to attend his clinics. He taught me the following exercise and had my young horse doing flying changes despite me being dubious about it at that age of the horse. The result was that the horse did magnificent changes without any mistakes for the rest of his life.

That clinic was 4 days long, and, after 2 days, Karl decided to teach three 15-16 year old Prix St. Georges horses piaffe, much to the three owners' delight! To my amazement he taught and achieved reasonably good piaffes with these three horses, each by a different method in those two days and that really blew my mind.

About a year or two later, Nuno Oliveira came to this country [Australia]. Begining with the Karl Mikolka clinic, followed by the 8 or 9 yeas that Nuno Oliveira taught us, I experience an incredible learning curve.

Preparation for flying changes

You must be confident of the strike-off to each collected canter, both true canter and contra canter.

So do your collected canter strike-off from the walk giving a small but clear and definite kick with your outside leg, repeat all around the *manège* and on circles and the diagonals.

Mix up the canters - true, true, false, true, false, false, true, true, true, false, true, false, false and so on. [Here, *false* canter means *contra canter* or *counter canter*]. Sounds a bit odd but really makes sure you and your horse are 110% sure about walk, correct canter strike-off, walk.

This, plus the quality of the canter are the priorities for a flying change. The horse must change legs [lead] in the air, during the moment of suspension in the canter stride.

You need to give the aid just before this moment and you need to learn to feel "when."

This is not as difficult as it sounds because that moment is in the 'flat spot' of each canter stride.

The other principle is to do these flying changes early in your horse's career. It is a natural movement to a horse so do it as soon as his canter is round and balanced and teach the flying change when your strike-offs are totally correct, every time.

An exercise to teach your horse a single flying change

This was the exercise Karl Mikolka used to teach my very young horse his flying changes.

Remember your priorities:

>Roundness - Rhythm - Straightness.

As in diagram A, trot across the diagonal, near M, walk two to three steps hindquarters in and then trot forward correctly through the corner. Repeat two or three times.

Then collected canter (right) across the diagonal, at the same place before M, trot two to three steps in hindquarters-in, and then canter (left) through the corner correctly. Repeat two to three times.

When the canter section of diagram B has been done calmly and with confidence, then again, canter across the diagonal, but do not trot on approaching M, instead, sit in deeper, flex your fingers and quickly, firmly and lightly a clear tap with the new outside leg (right) behind the girth in the flat moment of the canter stride, and your horse will do his first flying change.

Fantastic! Stop, drop the reins, and pat him.

If the change does not happen repeat the exercise. Do not punish him. If you do, he will always be frightened of flying changes, and do them with tension.

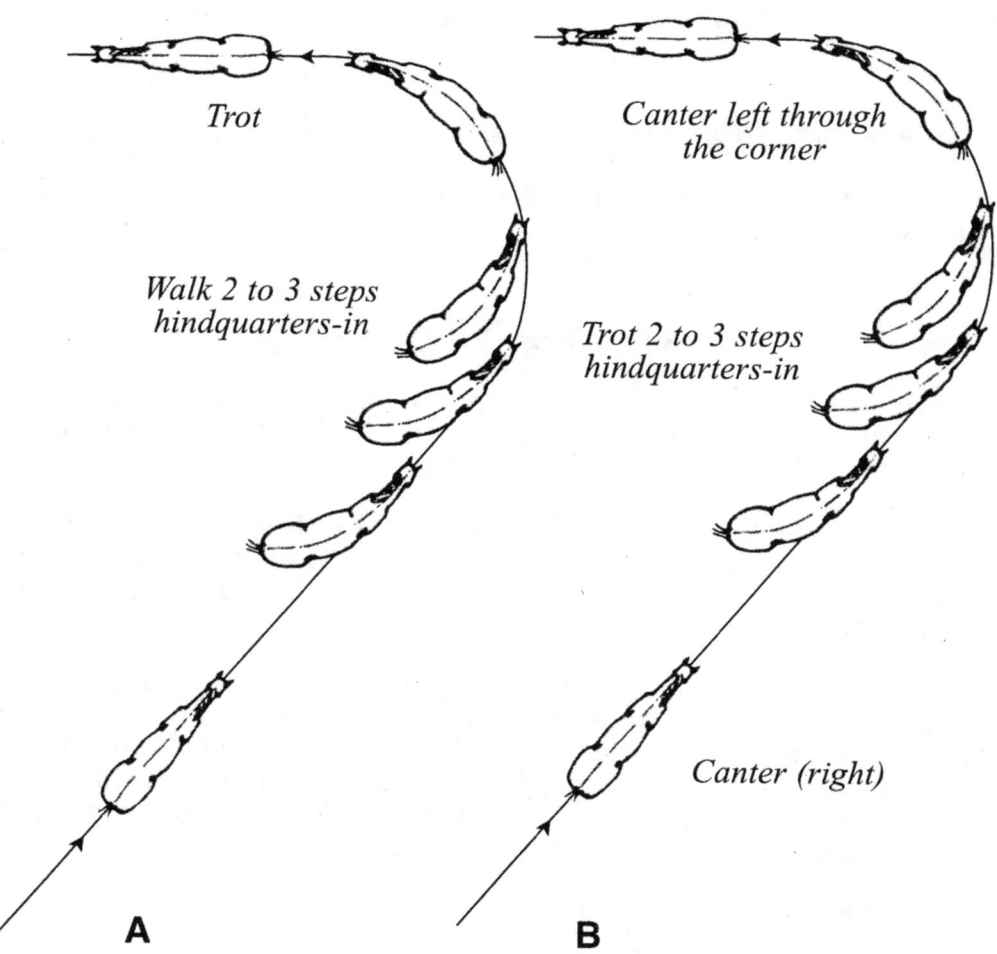

If all is relaxed and calm, and the change achieved, repeat one more time then repeat the exercise in the other direction, remembering to keep the horse's canter tempo unchanged, the horse straight, and asking for the change from your leg not your hand!

When the horse changes, reward him immediately, pat him, give him carrots or sugar, tell him he is wonderful, and put him back in the stable.

To practice the change once your horse knows how to do them, you can use a half *volte* and a short track back to the long side and flying change as you come to the wall. Doing lots of changes in different places will make both you and your horse confident with the changes.

This is another way to teach flying changes.

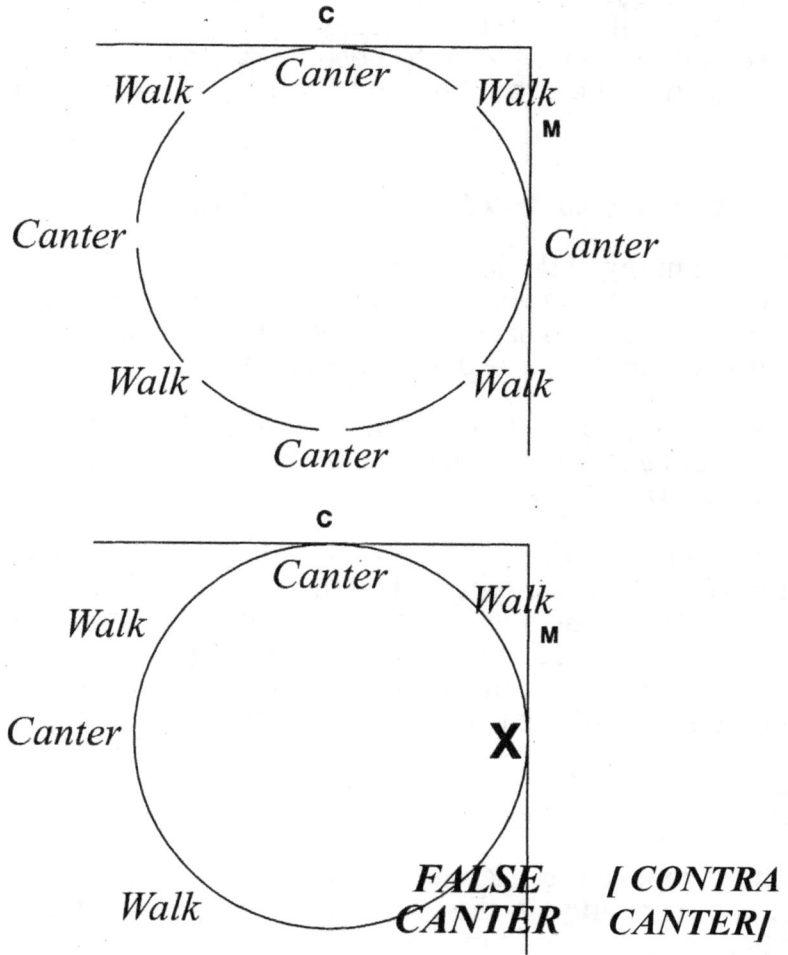

Prepare your horse, make sure the collected canter is light and cadenced and round and do some canter strike-offs, from walk and back to walk with only a few strides of canter each time.

[Give a] clear definite tap / kick with your new outside leg for every strike-off.

About 3, 4 circles gives about 9 - 12 strike-offs. Look at the second diagram on the previous page, and ask for the false [counter] canter after the center line.

After 2 or 3 strides of false [contra] canter, as you approach the wall give your aids and ask for a flying change.

Be patient and think through the aid sequence so you have it clear in your mind and then give the aid to change legs [lead] in the flat spot in the canter stride.

When teaching flying changes don't ever become cross and don't upset your horse if he doesn't get it right. Whips etc. will only make him tense and he could [learn to become] always tense for a long time afterward. So be patient and if necessary try a different way.

Another exercise to teach the flying change

At the beginning of the long side (for example, at H) about four to five meters from the corner from the walk, contra canter four to five strides, then walk. Turn back to the short side in walk and repeat the same transition in the same place several times.

If this is all completed in a calm and relaxed manner and the horse's canter remains round, then put the horse in a true canter near C on the track towards H.

Canter (true canter) - go well into the corner (before H) and with the horse very straight, light and round and the rider sitting very straight and still, at the place where you were doing the transitions to counter canter, do a brief tighten of your fingers and at the same time a very quick and definite tap with your new outside leg (the leg is on the inside of the track to give you contra canter).

If your horse has done his first flying change stop, drop the reins, and reward him.

Carefully repeat the exercise at the other end and when you have one flying change in the other direction, get off, make much of your horse, and put him in the stable!!
WOW! IT HAPPENED!

He changed legs [leads] and everything was straight and calm and his canter stayed the same. Stop, drop the reins and make much of him. Pat him, tell him he's wonderful, give him sugar etc. and then go back and establish the canter and straight away do it again and repeat the rewards. Next, carefully try the other side.

YOU GOT IT AGAIN!

Wonderful! Lots of rewards and this time get off and finish for the day with huge pats and rewards.

HELP! IT DIDN'T HAPPEN

* **He didn't change, just got faster.** You must sit up, sit in, and flex your fingers almost half-halt as you give the aid. All this in a quick sequence so you have to think it through quite a few times so you can do it.

* **He pig-rooted or kicked out.** Your outside leg was probably too far back and the kick too strong. It has to be a clear definite quick kick but be careful, sometimes riders can get frustrated and the spur ends up in the horse's flank.

* **He was late behind but he got it together after 2 or 3 strides.** Young horses often do this, don't panic, he will probably get it right fairly soon. You must keep calm and give the aids in the sequence and ask in the same place in the *manège* each time. Also if you're not sure if he's half or one stride late behind, ask someone to watch at this time and whenever he's right and gets it altogether [united], [give him] lots of pats, lots of rewards.

* **He's swinging his quarters in the flying change.** This needs to be corrected now or he'll swing his quarters when doing multiple tempi changes. Do your changes along a wall; change from true to false canter so he has to stay straight. Pay particular attention to the horse's straightness in his everyday canter work. Go back to the exercise in the chapter on collection [riding on the quarter-lines in contra canter to re-prove that he is straight]. Remember about riding the straight line slightly shoulder-fore to place the shoulders in front of the hindquarters to make your horse straight.

Your feeling in all changes should be uphill and with expression not a flat change that you can barely feel.

If he doesn't get it right don't get upset, it will make your horse tense about the flying changes. Ask for some help from a trainer who is good at flying changes.

An exercise that may help is to canter across the diagonal and after X, keep the canter but change the flexion (flexion not bend) to the new leg. Then after several strides nearer the wall ask for the change. Be careful to vary the number of strides between changing the flexion and asking the flying change so that the horse doesn't learn to change to the new inside rein but only changes to the new outside leg.

* **Your horse is changing true and correct but only some strides after you give the aid.** This is unlikely to happen if during his training you have insisted he react to your aids when you give them at that moment, not in his time! Go back and make sure his canter strike-off is exactly when you ask it [and not a second or two after you ask].

* **He's getting excited and anticipating the change.** Simply don't do it. Just ride different lines with no change, have a transition to trot and do a circle or a walk. Do something else, something different and then restart the canter. Your horse must remain calm before you do a flying change.

* **It has ruined your contra canter**! Yes, you have to be able to do your contra canter correctly. Remember to confirm the canter lead by a TINY kick just behind the girth on every stride. Take care not to move your leg too far back so your horse doesn't misinterpret your aid, and [end up doing, unwanted] travers!

* **He sort of stopped, hesitated then jumped through the change.** Be sure your canter is rhythmic and regular and take care with your hands: don't give a big half-halt before the change. Ride him more forward afterwards. Only change legs when you are both relaxed and calm and STRAIGHT in the canter.

If everything fails you can always teach a flying change in the air over a small jump. Can be difficult for the rider because you have to give a small clear kick with your new outside leg in the middle of the jump and also land going in the new direction so the horse changes legs [lead].

Then, when you are confident, you lower the jump and keep lowering it so he is still doing his change over a very low pole. Then, take the pole away.

When you can do your flying change at the end of the diagonal or along the long side you could try two changes on the long side then the diagonal. The diagonal is more difficult as you have to be careful to be straight.

To do two changes on a 20 meter circle is more difficult, but if you keep your horse very straight on the circle, and in a light canter, you will do it, and then try four changes.

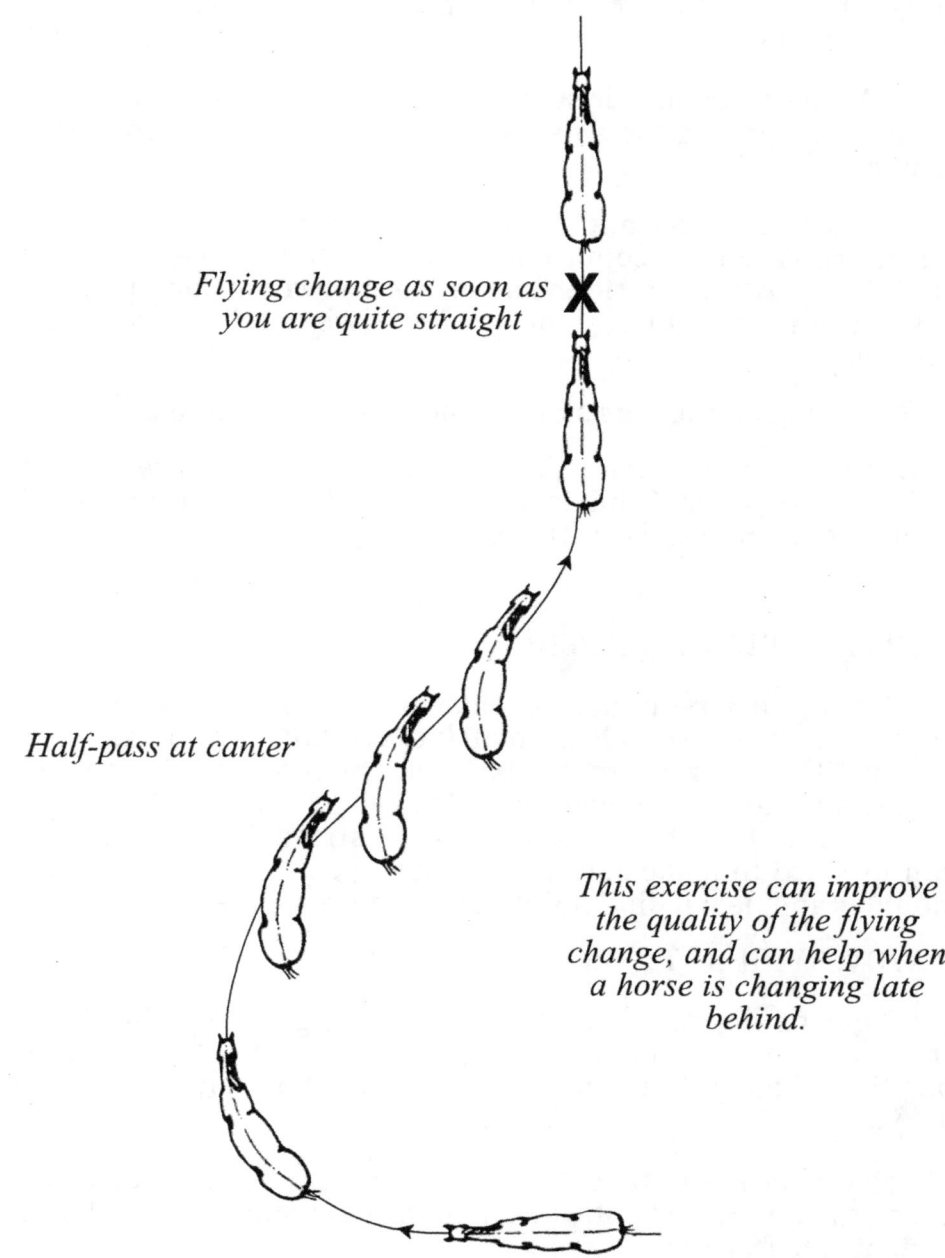

Flying change as soon as you are quite straight

Half-pass at canter

This exercise can improve the quality of the flying change, and can help when a horse is changing late behind.

Tempi changes

Changes every stride are not difficult for the horse once the single changes are correct and can be done anywhere and EXACTLY when the aid is given.

Most problems arise with the riders who have trouble counting and giving the aids all in sequence coordinated with the correct number.

Most trainers want to help and count out loud for the rider, but the rider should count out loud as well. One day, the trainer won't be there so the rider has to learn to count for themselves. You can practice counting the stride before you begin adding the changes.

Beginning on the long side will help keep him straight.

Begin down the long side with 2 changes, the second on the fourth stride or if this is all too quick for you, be imaginative and begin on the sixth stride.

HELP! IT DIDN'T HAPPEN!

* **He was a stride late.** Make sure you have him straight and sit up, sit in, and give a clear, small kick with the new outside leg as you say "3" to yourself, in the flat spot. The moment of suspension is next and he can change, to your kick on the fourth stride. So learn to count in the flat spot of each stride. Remember not to lean forward to make sure he's changed, if you do you'll load his shoulder and he will find it difficult to complete the change.

WOW! YOU GOT IT RIGHT!

* Now it's all just a matter of remembering to keep him straight, sit up, sit in, give your aid and keep counting and you can do lots of four-time changes but, not to the false [counter] canter in a corner, just yet.

Remember not to take the new inside rein before each change. Yes, he can be VERY slightly flexed to the new canter lead but totally straight is better!

If you always take the new inside rein before every change and then kick, your horse will learn this as an early change aid.

Straight is the most important prerequisite.

Now nothing will stop you!

When you are confident and your horse is doing super, straight changes every 4th stride, begin to do them every 3rd stride and then every 2nd. Sometime later, when these are all calm, straight and correct you can think about one time changes.

The late, great Nuno Oliveira taught me from the ground to teach my horse one time changes when I'd never ridden them. I thought this was pretty clever of him because it happened immediately: 2 one time changes, and then again, and then we repeated in the other direction, and then lots of sugar and back to the stable.

The preparation had been done in the five months between clinics. Go home and 2 maybe 3 times per week do different timed changes, some 4's, some 2's, no 3's. Next time, some 2's and some 3's, so that the horse and rider were totally confident and did not mix them up. Not doing 4's then 3's then 2's like it so often happens.

The one times began with the same canter, walk, canter, halt transitions and some 2 x changes and then along the wall in collected canter VERY straight. Flying change and the aid for the next change before the first change was complete and *VOILA* he did it!

To give the aid, put both legs a little behind the girth so that you can give each aid with the smallest of movement and effort from the rider. Swinging legs and twisting bodies will make it difficult for the horse.

There is an old video with Henri St. Cyr doing one time changes and nothing moves, he just sits there straight, still and elegant! Then he changes to passage and still nothing moves with the rider! Whenever your horse makes a mistake with tempi changes on a diagonal, go back and repeat on the same diagonal in the same direction. The horse must get it right on the diagonal where you ask. Don't allow the mistake on one diagonal and then get it right (corrected) on the next different diagonal [coming from the other direction]. If this happens several times, your horse just might learn which diagonal he can make mistakes on.

After two days of 2 one time changes, we progressed to 3, one time changes and then 4. At 5 the horse was finding it easy. Nuno Oliveira said do not ask for a lot more at this early stage. If you get overconfident when the horse looks as if he could do 15 easily this early in his learning, "that is when you are likely to lose a hind leg [the horse might not change behind, only in front] and you won't feel it."

As a precaution, try to [always] have someone watch [from the ground] to make sure the changes are true.

The other precaution is to decide once more, before you begin, exactly how many changes you aim to do. Don't get near the end of 9 changes for example, and then on the eighth change think about doing a few more because it's all going well. You may hesitate in your aid and unintentionally unbalance your horse. Finish the nine, lots of rewards and when you repeat decide, once more, before you begin how many, sometimes more, sometimes only a few, not always the same number just because he can do it.

After each lesson of one time changes be sure to do some 2's, 3's or 4's for your horse, just a few to finish with so you don't put him back into the stable with one time changes in his head.

Piaffe and Passage

Piaffe and Passage

Which one first?

Mostly you teach piaffe first but sometimes a horse doesn't understand and offers passage so change your aids and let him do his first steps of passage.

Aids? Aids for piaffe and passage can differ from instructor / rider to another instructor.

Some horses react better to alternate legs for passage and a gentle rhythmic elastic touch from both legs together in the trot rhythm for piaffe.

This gives them a clear difference of aids to obtain the different [types of] trot, for that, of course, is what piaffe and passage are [different types of trot].

The important points are that your horse sits a little in his collection, in his own balance, that you don't use the whip as the primary aid but only to give brilliance to the movement.

Always remember to stop both piaffe and passage *before* the *horse* wants to stop. This is strenuous on the horse. Do not do so much that he becomes over-tired.

If you wish to teach piaffe in hand first, get some help from a trainer who is experienced with this and then get on your horse and ask with your back, seat and legs, then spur (gently), then whip as a last aid IF you need it.

Remember to sit still and allow the horse to move underneath you.

HELP!

* **Your horse is bouncing in front doing little half rears.** Allow him to do tiny steps (creep) forward a little and LESS contact from the rider[the reins]. The hand only closes the door in front of the horse, and then gives to allow the horse to move in his own balance.

* **Your horse is evading sideways, swinging his hindquarters.** Again, allow the horse to creep forward in little tiny steps and keep the shoulders in front of his hindquarters. Check your contact which must be light so the horse can piaffe in his own balance.

   * **The horse doesn't lift his legs in diagonal [pairs]**. Here is where work in-hand can help, or go back a training step and use a shorter and shorter trot and ask for less steps on the spot 1, 2 or 3 and again forward in the short trot.

   * **Your halt and salute is anticipating piaffe.** Don't do piaffe on the center line often, especially not where it is asked for in a test. Use the diagonal and the quarter lines and also make short lines across the arena. Use your imagination.

   Your piaffe can improve in several ways.

   The usual way is by asking for piaffe pirouettes.

   Another way to improve the "sit" is by doing your piaffe on a small downward slope. Your horse has to "sit" to do this and this exercises all the joints in the hind legs as he has to flex them more to do piaffe on this small slope.

   The important point is that the horse learns to do, as with all things, what you ask, where you ask and when you ask. Even more important is that he stops and relaxes when you ask so that you can halt without him offering piaffe or a rein-back or passage.

   You are the boss!!

   When confirmed and confident, piaffe is an excellent gymnastic exercise, not only good for the 'sit,' flexing of hind legs, but also good for the horse's back as he rounds it into the 'sit' for collection.

Passage comes from a more active shorter trot with frequent half-halts.

To begin on a small volte quarters-in the horse can offer small indications of passage and you will immediately reward these true pre-passage steps with sugar, etc. Giving your aid of alternate little touches / kicks in the trot rhythm can help him.

A few, not many attempts with indications like this, and he can go back to the stable with lots of rewards for being so good and for trying.

With patience, often in a surprisingly short time you will get some passage steps, again lots of rewards and finish for the day.

Patience and lack of whips will develop a passage without tension, in his own balance, and it will be magic to sit on.

HELP!

* My passage is unlevel but my horse is quite regular in the other trot movements. Teaching passage using alternate leg aids can help avoid an aid unintentionally encouraging more effort from one diagonal. Your hands can interfere, the horse must passage in his own balance. Then there are whips! Too much use of a whip can cause irregularity in the passage and NEVER should you use the whip on one side of the horse only, you must change the whip, remembering a whip is the last aid.

If you are patient with your horse after he has learned passage and don't resort to a whip for more height in the passage, as he gets stronger and more confidence, by you shortening the steps a little he will become higher.

You can encourage these slightly shorter and higher steps and gradually develop them with patience and lots of rewards.

Your horse now has all Grand Prix movements, he is supple, athletic and obedient. He carries himself in his own balance, your aids are feather light and your rapport with him is such that he is a pleasure to ride, so that when you get off you want to get back on again, you enjoyed it so much.

www.ingramcontent.com/pod-product-compliance
Lightning Source LLC
Chambersburg PA
CBHW060514300426
44112CB00017B/2672